The Sandusky, Mansfield & Newark Railroad

Early History of
the Lake Erie Division of the B&O

Second Edition

Fig. 1. B&O Enginie #978.

The Sandusky, Mansfield & Newark Railroad

Early History of
the Lake Erie Division of the B&O

Second Edition

by

Robert A. Carter

The Sandusky, Mansfield

& Newark Railroad

Early History of

the Lake Erie Division of the B&O

Second Edition

by

Robert A. Carter

ISBN 978-1-7361884-8-4

TURAS PUBLISHING

This is our history - from the Transcontinental Rail-road to the Hoover Dam, to the dredging of our ports and building of our most historic bridges - our American ancestors prioritized growth and investment in our nation's infrastructure.

Cory Booker

Table of Contents

List of Figures

List of Figures - *Continued*

Introduction

Very little has been written about that little north - south railroad that shot straight south across the prairie flat lands of Erie and Huron Counties, snaked its way through the twisting valleys of Richland and meandered among the rolling hills of Knox and Licking Counties. A half dozen separate railroad starts, none of which were profitable and doomed to failure, were blended into one final effort, the Sandusky Mansfield & Newark Railroad Company. This book is a brief study of the need, the obstacles, and the never ending challenges faced by those who built and those who ran the first railroad in North Central Ohio.

A mild interest in the SM&N RR started in the 1970s upon locating several old locomotive photographs with crew standing along side. These were the iron men who road the wooden trains, braved the dangers and foul weather, worked long hours for little pay, and had pride in what they accomplished.

Research turned out to be a puzzle. Various county histories all told the same story, several copied or written by the same author. The railroads Annual Reports were the best source of specific information. These reports, written by the president and heads of transportation and maintenance, were a condensed record of each year's activities. These were found at the Ohio Historical Library in Columbus, the Western Reserve Historical Library in Cleveland, and the greatest amount at the Hayes Presidential Library in Fremont. The staffs at Columbus and Cleveland were most helpful and patient with my requests, and Mervin Hall, of the Hayes Library, went out of his way to locate what this amateur was looking for. From the library stacks he brought forth records I hadn't asked for and didn't realize they had. Several items the library had not yet cataloged. I am most grateful for his assistance.

Another key source was the newspaper files. Early issues were often scattered and incomplete, but endless hours spent with micro film files filled the empty spots that didn't make the annual reports. They provided the community background, both political and business, with which the railroad was involved in some way. The Sandusky papers were the chief source of information. The railroad offices and shops were there, as was the newspaper editor's interest over the years.

The Mansfield papers were more political than anything, carried very little local news, and seldom mentioned the railroads. The *Newark Advocate*, the city's leading paper, was against building another railroad (they had already started the Central Ohio) and unless there was a wreck or flood, contained very little. Smaller competing papers did report on the road, but issues are scattered. The Mt. Vernon papers were much better balanced, covering business and the railroad. Oddly enough, I found the Monroeville newspaper files are not in Monroeville. They're in the Milan Public Library. Most small towns along the SM&N didn't have newspapers until after the turn of the century.

The Willard Public Library has a wonderful railroad photographic collection but would not permit publication for commercial use. This limited edition book is a labor of love and will never show a profit what with today's Internet systems. All to often the well intended folks that look after local museums and libraries are elderly, a decade behind in thought, and more concerned with protection than education. Volunteers to staff most small town institutions are difficult to find, limiting access.

The Garrett Hayes Coleman Photographic Collection at the Ohio Historical Center Library is a marvelous collection of railroad pictures. The Society's permission to use them for this publication is greatly appreciated.

The Railroad Annual Reports were already condensed. Something was lost in reducing them further, and many selections are quoted as written. The same problems seemed to crop up year after year. It must be appreciated that in most cases only one copy of these reports is known to exist! They are extremely rare! They are all that is left of the railroad. They are, after all, its history.

The newspapers were also dated and quoted as written even though sentences at times seem to go on forever. In rewriting these stories I found the flavor and language of the times was often lost. I left them as an editor or reporter set them down with pen and ink. It seemed more interesting that way, even if I had to sometimes read them twice.

A special thanks to my youngest son, Robert W. Carter, an engineer with NASA, who agreed to assemble my manuscript and rectify all the places his father had totally murdered the King's English. It probably saved it from becoming a family embarrassment.

Bob Carter
July, 2002

Chapter 1
Sandusky, Mansfield & Newark Railroad

The 1820s and 30s were a difficult period for those living in what might best described as North Central Ohio. The economy was based on agriculture. The pioneer farms and water powered gristmills, which had earlier provided enough to support those families hardy enough to carve out homesteads in the wilderness, began to produce surplus crops of grain, live stock, and flour. Economic problems developed stemming from the fact that only a limited local market existed for these surpluses. Lack of a national currency exacerbated the situation. *Wildcat Banks*, that is, banks that were founded without a State Charter, went into business, printed their own currency, and often failed. The German Bank of Wooster, the Richland and Huron Bank of Mansfield, and the Owl Creek Bank of Mount Vernon all collapsed. Because of bank failures all paper money was viewed with suspicion. The result was an economy based to a large extent on the barter system. What little cash money existed often was not worth its face value, or was totally worthless. For a brief period the Richland County Treasurer at Mansfield was forced to accept produce for payment of taxes.

The solution to these economic problems lay in Eastern markets, or cities down the Ohio River. Here goods could be exchanged for a more reliable currency, manufactured goods, salt, or other commodities needed in the frontier communities. However, the difficulty involved in reaching these points was a great hardship on all those who dared make the trip.

Heavy wide wheeled wagons loaded with wheat, corn, flour, and whisky (it was easier to ship a barrel of whisky than a load of corn), were seen driving across hills, through unbridged streams and rivers, and snaking along deep rutted axle breaking excuses for roads. Ten miles a day was considered good progress with a four horse team. Dust choked the teamsters in dry weather, mud buried them in wet. In other attempts flat boats loaded with produce were launched at Loudenville and Perrysville bound down river for New Orleans (a perilous journey that could take a month). And then there was the long trip back on foot or horseback. There had to be a better way.

Sandusky had a natural harbor, and by 1834 locks had been built on the Huron River enabling canal boats to reach a point near Milan. The boats then passed down the canal to the lake port of Huron where their cargo was reloaded onto lake sailing vessels for shipment to eastern markets via the Erie Canal. The success of this venture prompted the Canal Company's directors to widen and deepen the waterway so that by 1839 lake schooners could reach the canal basin at the edge of Milan. Business boomed, warehouses went up, and for a brief period Milan was the greatest port for grain shipments in the United States. A plank road was built south a few miles to aid teamsters with their heavy wagons which often sank into the soft prairie soil.

This did little for Sandusky's expansion, and the need for inland transportation remained unsolved. The success of the Erie Canal in New York spurred capitalists and legislators in Ohio to develop a plan for inland canals to connect Lake Erie to the Ohio River.

Cleveland and Sandusky both lobbied the State Legislature for a southern canal route. Cleveland got the nod. The Sanduskians cried foul, claiming political maneuvering and underhanded dealings, which is exactly what happened. Never the less a grand groundbreaking for the Ohio Canal took place on July 4, 1825 at a point called *Licking Summit*, about four miles from Newark. Work on the canal began at once, but would require several years of back breaking work and enormous cost to complete. The route from Cleveland was up the Cuyahoga River through Akron, and down the Tuscarawas River to Massillon, Dover, New Philadelphia, Coshocton, and Dresden. At Dresden it turned up the Licking River to Newark before continuing south to Portsmouth on the Ohio River. The first canal boat from Cleveland arrived in Newark on August 21, 1830.

The prospect of having canal boats in Newark on the Ohio and Erie Canal was a tremendous asset to Licking County and those fortunate enough to live near the waterway. But for Mt. Vernon, thirty miles to the north in Knox County, and Mansfield in Richland County roughly sixty miles from either Newark or Lake Erie, little benefit could be seen. The north eastern part of Ohio would prosper while the north central section remained mired in mud.

Pressure was applied for months and State Legislators reluctantly caved in and authorized the construction of a feeder canal from Roscoe, across the river from Coshocton. This branch would go up the Walhonding and Mohican rivers to Loudenville, a distance of 50 miles. There was some hope that it might reach Ganges in Richland County, a distance of 75 miles. Similar canals from the Walhounding up the

Kokosing to Mt. Vernon, or up the Killbuck to Millersburg, were also considered, but only the Walhounding and Mohican Canal, as it was named, was approved. Construction started in 1837 just as a financial panic hit the nation. The state could not appropriate the funds needed according to plans causing delays and sometimes halting work.

Part of the unfinished canal finally opened in June of 1842 for a distance of 25 miles. The canal passed through the small towns of Walhounding and Warsaw to reach the settlements of Cavallo and Rochester, which were across the Mohican from each other in a deep valley with limited access. This was as far as it would ever go. Historians have referred to the canal as *twenty five miles to nowhere*, which is an accurate statement. Rochester and Cavallo, where warehouses and a mill were built in hopes of a bright future, have virtually disappeared. The canal was a $607,268 failure. For years to come tolls would not cover operational and maintenance costs. One account estimates that an average of only one boat a month passed through it.

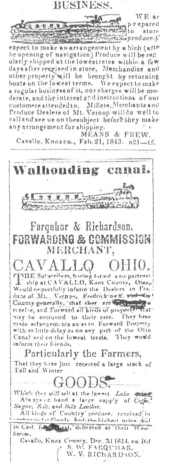

Fig. 2. Left: The Walhonding Canal had reached a point 25 miles upstream in 1842. It would end at Cavallo and Rochester, both of which had high hopes for freight traffic that never materialized. The State refused to fund any further extension.

Chapter 2
Could There Be a Better Way?

The February 21, 1829 issue of the *Norwalk Reflector* carried a story originally published in the *Western Aurora*, a Mt. Vernon newspaper. The lengthy article suggested a possible solution. The following excerpt is from the Norwalk Reflector:

> *In the Aurora, the attention of the public was called to the subject of Rail Roads and Canals, with a view towards the location of one of the two through our rich valley, as a means of exporting its produce, and affording sufficient inducement for turning the wild forest into a valuable cultivated region.*
>
> *Several intelligent and enterprising gentlemen in Huron, Richland, Knox, Licking, Muskingum, Morgan and Washington Counties, have been conversed on the subject since that time. The practicability and general advantages of a continuation of the Baltimore Railway from Marietta up the valley of the Muskingum River, Licking, Owl, and Mohican creeks, and on down the valley of the Huron River, to the dividing ridge between that and Sandusky River to the Lake; has been admitted to.*
>
> *An intelligent practical Engineer has estimated the general ascent of the valley from Marietta to Zanesville, Newark, and Mt. Vernon, to be a fraction more than two feet per mile.....From Mansfield to Portland (Sandusky), the country is thought to average about three feet per mile.*

The Baltimore and Ohio Railroad was planning a line west through the Allegheny Mountains to reach the Ohio River in the early 1830s. News of this grand plan must have sent minds dreaming. It would be January 1853 before the first train would arrive on the Ohio River, but not at Marietta. Wheeling, West Virginia, was the point.

Sandusky, which had lost its canal bid to Cleveland, knew railroads were the answer if it was to keep its stature as a major lake port. After some foot dragging the State Legislature finally granted a charter for the Mad River and Lake Erie Railroad on January 5, 1832. A charter gave its directors permission to sell stock and acquire lands and property for a right of way. The proposed route was south-west from Sandusky through Bellevue and Tiffin, with a goal of reaching Springfield and a connection with the Little Miami Railroad and the Ohio River at Cincinnati.

This broke the ice, so to speak. A charter for a line from Sandusky to Monroeville was granted on March 9, 1835. One year later another was granted for a line north from Mansfield to New Haven in southern Huron County. This left a gap between the two roads from New Haven to Monroeville, which would somehow have to be filled for either to be successful. The solution was a merger of the Sandusky & Monroeville with the Mansfield & New Haven to form the Mansfield and Sandusky City Railroad.

Attorney James Purdy of Mansfield was among leading citizens involved in promoting the northern road. He wrote articles in local newspapers and appeared at lectures and meetings urging farmers and businessmen to purchase stock in the new corporation. He predicted trade and land values would increase several fold when the road opened.

In the April 4, 1840 edition of the *Richland Jeffersonian*, a Mansfield newspaper, Purdy wrote the following letter on the subject:

> *It is known that in order to reach the lake, our cars must pass over the Sandusky & Monroeville Rail Road. It became a matter of importance for our company to have an agreement on the subject. I was requested to draw up an agreement, which I did. At a meeting of the board, it was approved.*

Purdy went to Sandusky by horse and buggy, reached an agreement with the Sandusky group, and met some friends who were going to New York by boat. He went along with them as far as Syracuse where he wanted to inspect a railroad being built. Although he paid for the New York trip out of his own pocket the board thought his bill for expenses, a little over $19.00, was excessive.

Sandusky had its own leaders supporting stock sales and urging prompt action to prevent the establishment of a competing road from Norwalk to the port of Huron. Stock sales went well.

A grand ground breaking was held on September 17, 1835 at the Sandusky waterfront for both the Mad River & Lake Erie and the Sandusky & Monroeville Railroads. General William Henry Harrison turned the first shovel of dirt; speeches were made, including one by Eleutheros Cook, who had served terms in both the Ohio House and Senate. The Governor of Ohio also spoke. Cannons fired, toasts were offered, and a crowd estimated at a thousand celebrated well into the evening. A banquet was held at the Victor Hotel, where the event included a party of Wyandot Indians. The Mad River & Lake Erie was to pass through part of their reservation near Upper Sandusky and the road's Board of Directors didn't want any trouble.

Chapter 3

Construction Begins

Details of early roadbed efforts are sketchy. The Mad River & Lake Erie line made the most progress with the Sandusky & Monroeville coming in second. The *Norwalk Register* reported in its July 3, 1838 edition that an ivory like tusk, 10 feet long and measuring 9 inches at the base, had been unearthed at *Slate Run*, about five miles south of Sandusky in a deep cut. The roadbed was basically all wood, with an 8 X 12 mud sill laid down on grade. Cross ties were laid across the sills and 4 X 6 wooden rails topped with a 2 ½ inch wide by 5/8 inch thick iron strap rail, were laid on the ties. The line was open to Monroeville by September of 1838 with cars drawn by horses. A siding six and a half miles from Sandusky allowed cars to pass and also change horses. The cars were four wheeled open box cars with a tarp covering loads. A primitive passenger car had been fabricated and the 12.8 mile passenger trip took about 2 ½ hours behind tandem hitched teams. Freight loads sometimes took much longer.

The line operated under heavy expenses and only lasted 31 months. At the end, 24 horses were able to pull cars, 8 had been killed, and 6 sold. The line was supposed to cost $100,000 to build, but it was claimed that it had only cost a little over $43,000. When the interest wasn't paid on a $33,333.33 State loan, Ohio sold the line to the then un-built Mansfield and New Haven Railroad for $33,333.33 in their stock on May 25, 1843.

A story in the July 25, 1845, *Sandusky Clarion*, under the heading *Mansfield and Sandusky City Railroad*, gave a brief history of events:

> *A few years ago, a company was chartered to make a railroad from this place to Monroeville. The road was made but not in a very substantial manner. There was a good deal of business done upon it but at heavy expense, as the transportation was by horse power. The stock decreased in value, and the road was finally sold by the state for its lien, although it took stock to the amount of its claim under the new charter.*

It was bought by a company of which Mr. Burr Higgins, of this city, is the principal agent and manager. Since then perfect confidence has been felt, not only in the speedy completion of the road, and in the liberal profits to be realized by the enterprising stockholders....There has been a very heavy expenditure at this place for a depot, being all built on man made land in the bay, extending from shore into deep water. The walls of the building are up, and are, like the road, built in the most substantial manner.

Some time ago, a new locomotive, called the "Mansfield," arrived and has, for a few weeks past, been running for purposes connected with construction of the road; but not until now has the business of carrying passengers recommenced, which was suspended during the reconstruction of the road.

On March 11, 1843 the Ohio General Assembly authorized the Ohio Board of Public Works to sell the Monroeville and Sandusky City Railroad Company provided that the Mansfield and New Haven Railroad Company, being the purchaser, certain rights and privileges should accrue to the company, including the right to change its corporate title. The new name would be the Mansfield & Sandusky City Railroad Company.

Burr Higgins was a prosperous mill owner from Castalia, Ohio. He had started a merchandise business at Venice at the mouth of Cold creek in 1834, and later went into milling at Castalia, where he eventually gained control of water rights and 500

Fig. 3. All that was left of the original Mansfield and Sandusky City Station after the June 1924 tornado. Burr Higgins well built station was just that, well built. Photo courtesy Hayes Presidential Library.

acres of land. The unfailing water from the underground spring (the Blue Hole) made his mills prosper. In 1836 he and several associates bought the charter of the first bank formed at Norwalk, in Huron County, after it had repaid its investors and closed.

The new engine *Mansfield* was no doubt patterned after the very first locomotive the firm of Rogers Ketchum & Grovsenor built. Named the *Sandusky*, it had been sold to the Mad River and Lake Erie Railroad in 1837 and arrived in Sandusky on November 17. No track had been laid to place it on. The directors wanted to make sure the track would match the wheel spacing, the distance between the rails a 4' 10" gauge. A full size model of the *Sandusky* mounted on original pieces of strap rail is on display in the Railroad Museum in Bellevue, Ohio.

The *Mansfield* was a small single driver engine weighing about 9 tons. It apparently had a 4-2-0 wheel arrangement (some sources claim 4-2-2, but Rogers engines of that era usually had no trailing truck) and had 10 ½ X 18 inch cylinders with 54 inch single driver wheels. These drive wheels were cast with hollow spokes and counter balanced, a development of Mr. Rogers. A company catalog shows the engines with no cab or weather protection for the crew, but this could have been fabricated by the owner. Usually painted black, the finish was highly polished.

The Sandusky and Monroeville had been built on a 4' 10" gauge, but had deteriorated to the point where rebuilding the 12.8 mile line was necessary. C. W.

Fig. 4. The engine "Sandusky" was the first one built by Rogers, Grosvenor & Ketchum, for the Mad River and Lake Erie Railroad. A full size model is in the Railroad Museum in Bellevue, Ohio. Courtesy of the Coleman Collection, Ohio Historical Society.

Williams, Burr Higgins' engineer, formerly of the 5' 4" gauge St. Lawrence and Atlantic Railroad in Maine, persuaded Higgins and his bankers to adopt the 5' 4" gauge. He sighted the advantage of wider fire boxes and increased engine efficiency.

The same July 25 issue of the Sandusky paper carried another related story:

> *On Wednesday, a splendid new car calculated for fifty-six passengers, man-ufactured by Hart, Higam & Co. of Utica N. Y., arrived and was placed upon the road. On Thursday we availed ourselves of an invitation extended to our citizens by the superintendent, to take a pleasure trip to Monroeville, and it was indeed a pleasure trip. The new car has 28 double seats with a passage running the whole length between which was nearly filled with ladies, where they could sit as comfortably as they could rest on their own sofas in their own parlors. Beside this, there were several open cars which carried as many more.....By first of September next, it is expected that the road will be completed.*

On January 10, 1844 Burr Higgins, superintendent of the road, advertised in the *Sandusky Clarion* for 1600 tons of railroad iron,

> *...of American or imported iron, in flat bars of good quality, weighing 30 to 35 ton to the mile, to be delivered free of charge on the waters of the Hudson, at New York or Albany, or at Buffalo, at Portsmouth, Cleveland or Sandusky, Ohio; at Beaver on the Ohio River, or at some port in Lake Ontario, during the navigable season of 1844, and all by the month of September next, if practicable.*

The request for proposals asked prospective suppliers for, *the width and thickness of the bar and the kind of joint, along with their most favorable terms as to price and payment.* It was clear that the directors were not sure of what they needed.

The following November this ad appeared under the heading *Notice for Timber*:

> *Proposals will be received until the 20th of December for about 40,000 feet of various sizes and lengths of hewn timber, and 10,000 feet of round, deliverable in part during the winter, and all by the first of May, 1845, at the depot buildings of the Mansfield and Sandusky City Railroad Company, in Sandusky City.*

The roadbed required vast amounts of timber. Heavy timber sills were laid down with cross ties spiked across them. Next came timbers which were set into the cross ties to prevent their spreading, and a two inch strip of hardwood placed on top to which the iron strap rail was nailed down through. In effect it was a wooden rail with an iron top, similar to the old roadbed, even though iron rails were being introduced in the east.

As construction continued south from Monroeville a natural route would have taken the road through New Haven, then a thriving community in southern Huron County. In the early 1840s most of the wagon traffic headed for Milan or Sandusky passed through New Haven. As early as 1825 a petition to the State Legislature asked for a State Road from Columbus thru Newark, Mt. Vernon, Mansfield, New Haven to Sandusky. New Haven, was also the terminus of the Worthington to New Haven road. It had a tannery with a large shoe making business employing *40 or 50 men*, five dry goods stores, a foundry, a steam flour mill, a fanning mill, and a large scale ashery. Several taverns and inns provided for the teamsters and drovers whose rigs were said to have filled the town square to the point that it was difficult to cross from one side to the other.

In a letter dated May 6, 1845, addressed to John Gardiner, a banker and businessman from Norwalk, Sumner P. Webber wrote the following:

> *I have bought a warehouse in New Haven for the purpose of commencing the forward and commission business as soon as the Sandusky and Mansfield Railroad will be finished to that place, which will be on July or August next. My friends here advise me to connect with merchandising and I think myself that one would help the other. I have paid for the warehouse and it has taken all that I could raise except $300.00. I wish you to inform me whether I could get credit for say $4000 worth of goods and how long the time of credit will be given if at all..... I was raised in the vicinity of New Haven and can do as good business as any man there.*

Gardiner was educated in the east and came to Ohio when he was 16. He started clerking in a store and at age 18 took a position as a clerk in the only bank in Norwalk. The cashier died two months later, leaving Gardiner in charge of the bank until a successor was found. Six years later he left banking and went into the

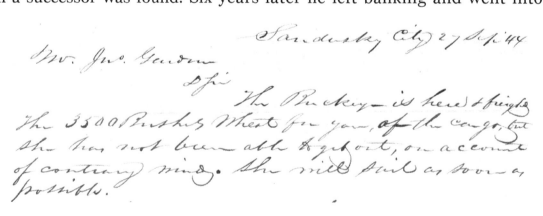

Fig. 5. John Gardiner was in the mercantile and produce business. A letter from a shipping firm advises; "The "Buckeye" is here & freighted the 3,500 bushels wheat for you of the cargo, but she has not been able to get out, on account of contrary wind. She will sail as soon as possible.

merchandising and produce business with considerable success, developing influential connections.Webber must have found what he wanted. He went into business but an ambush was waiting in the form of a local judge.

As the road was being built people were encouraged to invest or buy stock in the venture in order to raise the necessary capital needed for construction. Many did, but in New Haven a Judge Ives advised against any financial support, reasoning that the railroad would pass through the village anyway. Why not save your money? The tavern keepers, expecting a loss of their wagon customers, also voiced opposition against investing.

This must have put a burr under the saddle of Burr Higgins and his Board of Directors because they arched the line west through Havana and Centerton, by-passed New Haven by three quarters of mile, and continued on south to Plymouth, then a much smaller town. This spelled doom for Sumner Webber and most other New Haven business owners. When the road opened the town declined rapidly. When Judge Ives died in 1864 one could guess that there were few mourners at his funeral. The town was nearly deserted. Many buildings were abandoned, moved, or torn down. Few were left. Ironically, John Gardiner would later become President of the railroad that passed them by.

Two situations slowed construction at Plymouth, then known as Paris. A deep cut was required for the road to pass through. This would prove to be slow and labor intensive to dig. While this was being dug contractors leapfrogged ahead and continued south towards Shelby. All did not proceed smoothly however as the Sandusky paper reported of a meeting held in May of 1845;

> *There is some difficulty between the company and the citizens along the line beyond Paris, which may impede the progress of that part of the road. The origin of the difficulty is dissatisfaction at the allowance by the jury appointed by law to assess damages occasioned by the roads crossing lands of the citizens. We have heard that forcible means have been resorted to by the latter to stop the process of the work; and the resolution of a meeting accuse the company of giving sanction to the use of fire-arms with fixed bayonets, to drive the people from their possessions.*

The locomotive *Mansfield* made its maiden test trip the last week of April 1845, and was used to haul supplies as far south as Plymouth. Reloaded rail cars pulled by horses were used from that point on south through Shelby, Springmill, to Mansfield. Two more engines were delivered by ship in July of 1845, the *Empire* and the *Vigilance.*

The deep cut at Plymouth proved to be a bottleneck and was not finished until early in May of 1846. The first train from Sandusky to reach Mansfield did not arrive until May 16, 1846, although it may have stopped short of reaching town. A large crowd was on hand and a number of people went to Shelby or Springmill to ride on open cars to Mansfield. As the engine rolled into the gathering the engineer blew the whistle. The blast sent a shock wave through much of the crowd whom had never heard such a sound. A number of women fainted, fearing the thing would explode killing them or their children. It's possible a few men may have wet their pants as dogs barked and horses reared.

With the line finished there was a critical need for engines and equipment for the expected business. This story appeared in the July 14, 1846, edition of the *Sandusky Clarion* under the heading *New Locomotive*:

> *Another new locomotive from the manufactory of Messrs. Rogers, Ketchum & Grosvenor, of Patterson New Jersey, arrived on the brig Columbia, some days since, for the Mansfield and Sandusky City Rail-Road Company. It is about the same size as the "Mansfield" and is called the "Knox." The company now has four locomotives; the two mentioned above, the "Empire," and the "Vigilance."*

These single driver engines had to be shipped by canal boat on the Erie Canal to Buffalo N. Y. where they were loaded onto sailing ships for the passage across Lake Erie to Sandusky. There was no other way to deliver them. Getting them off the boat and onto the dock must have been interesting.

The Company was able to entice Thomas Hogg to leave the Mad River and Lake Erie and become the *Master of Machinery* for the Mansfield & Sandusky City Railroad. Hogg was born in England in 1808 where he learned the trade of machinist. When he came to America he worked for a number of years for Rogers, and came west to Ohio with the first locomotive Rogers built, the *Sandusky*, for the Mad River and Lake Erie. He set up the engine and was persuaded to remain as engineer. He went to work for the Mansfield & Sandusky City Railroad in 1846 and remained at that post for 21 years, retiring in 1867. He died at his farm near Danbury, in Ottawa County in 1881.

It's interesting to note that in an early accident on the Mad River line the *Sandusky* hit a cow near New Riegel in Seneca County and went off the tracks into the mud. It reportedly took, *two teams of oxen and a force of men*, to get it back on the rails. In cases of minor derailments passengers were sometimes requested to assist engine crews.

In the same July 14, 1846 issue the public was advised of regular freight and passenger service between Sandusky and Mansfield and all points between, including stage connections south to Columbus and Cincinnati. Passengers could leave Sandusky by train at 5:00 A.M. and reach Columbus by stage coach that same evening and Cincinnati at 10:00 A.M. the following day. Returning passengers would leave Mansfield at 4:00 P.M. and arrive in Sandusky at 7:00 PM. The total fare to Columbus was $4.50, Cincinnati $8.00, to Mansfield was only $1.75.

The June 18, 1846, edition of the *Cleveland Plain Dealer* carried a story about the new train and stage arrangements from Mansfield through Delaware to Columbus. It noted that the express company had changed its route by making Sandusky the point of leaving the lake instead of Cleveland. The editor must have felt a bit of envy as he wrote, *Our Sandusky friends are entitled to much credit for energy and dogged perseverance with which have carried on their road in spite of many obstacles.* The paper had been wondering why Cleveland had no rails and some business leaders felt that Sandusky might surpass them in a few years. The threat of railroads depleting canal traffic was beginning to worry them.

The August 4, 1846, edition of the *Sandusky Register* commented: *Such now are our facilities for traveling, that citizens from Cleveland find it most expeditious as well as the cheapest route, to take the steam boat to this place, to reach Mansfield and Columbus. The lines that stop here consist of six good steamers as follows; the Indiana, Troy, General Wayne, Bunker Hill, Chesapeake and General Harrison. We know of no instance of a boat leaving this port with less than twenty passengers, and in some instances, eighty to one hundred.*

Freight trains would leave Sandusky at 2:00 P.M. and Mansfield at 10:00 A.M. The freight cars were open top boxes which could hold 150 bushels of wheat or boxes and barrels of freight covered over with a tarpaulin. Merchandise or box cars would later be built by the company shops at Sandusky. These early cars were single axle but eight wheel cars with wooden trucks were adopted several years later.

Not much is known of the early success of the road. Limited operations in 1846 were greeted with enthusiasm by the directors and the public. A warehouse and dock were built at the lake in Sandusky, where Burr Higgins had his own forwarding business. In addition he built a grain warehouse over the tracks in Plymouth at the deep cut. This bridge-like affair allowed grain to be dumped into cars on the track below.

New structures were quickly constructed or converted in Monroeville by George Hollister. He began his career there with a distillery in 1825 - 26. It must have been successful, because he was on the Board of Directors of the first bank in Huron County. After selling the distillery he built a large warehouse and rail station.

The M&SC built a station at Fifth and Walnut in Mansfield, several warehouses and forwarding business were soon established by local businessmen. Other freight, or forwarding businesses as they were called, went up along the line. Shelby, Plymouth, and Centerton were quick to follow.

A financial report printed in the March 14, 1848, edition of the *Norwalk Reflector*, gives a nice history of the roads beginning:

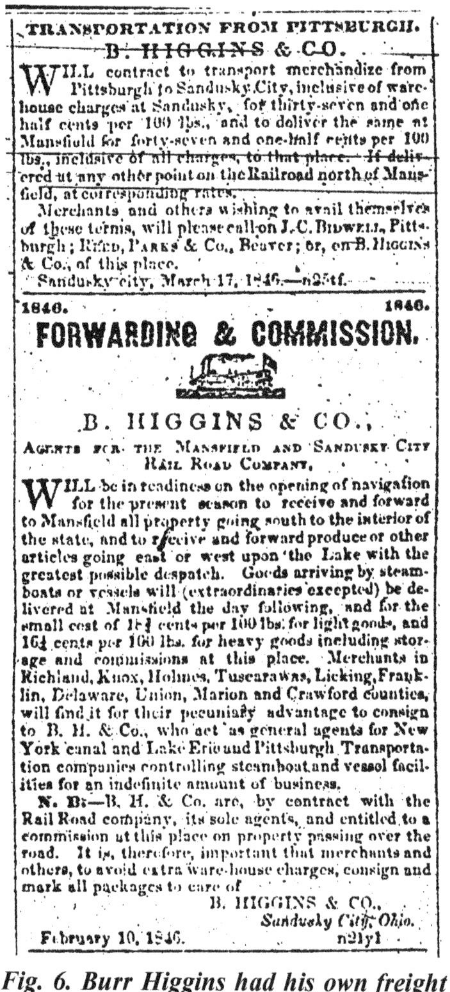

TRANSPORTATION FROM PITTSBURGH.
B. HIGGINS & CO.
WILL contract to transport merchandize from Pittsburgh to Sandusky City, inclusive of ware-house charges at Sandusky, for thirty-seven and one half cents per 100 lbs., and to deliver the same at Mansfield for forty-seven and one-half cents per 100 lbs., inclusive of all charges, to that place. If delivered at any other point on the Railroad north of Mansfield, at corresponding rates.
Merchants and others wishing to avail themselves of these terms, will please call on J. C. BIDWELL, Pittsburgh; REED, PARKS & Co., Beaver; or, on B. HIGGINS & Co., of this place.
Sandusky city, March 17, 1846.—n25tf.

1846. 1846.
FORWARDING & COMMISSION.
B. HIGGINS & CO.,
AGENTS FOR THE MANSFIELD AND SANDUSKY CITY RAIL ROAD COMPANY,
WILL be in readiness on the opening of navigation for the present season to receive and forward to Mansfield all property going south to the interior of the state, and to receive and forward produce or other articles going east or west upon the Lake with the greatest possible despatch. Goods arriving by steamboats or vessels will (extraordinaries excepted) be delivered at Mansfield the day following, and for the small cost of 18¾ cents per 100 lbs. for light goods, and 16¼ cents per 100 lbs. for heavy goods including storage and commissions at this place. Merchants in Richland, Knox, Holmes, Tuscarawas, Licking, Franklin, Delaware, Union, Marion and Crawford counties, will find it for their pecuniary advantage to consign to B. H. & Co., who act as general agents for New York canal and Lake Erie and Pittsburgh Transportation companies controlling steamboat and vessel facilities for an indefinite amount of business.
N. B.—B. H. & Co. are, by contract with the Rail Road company, its sole agents, and entitled to a commission at this place on property passing over the road. It is, therefore, important that merchants and others, to avoid extra ware-house charges, consign and mark all packages to care of
B. HIGGINS & CO.,
Sandusky City, Ohio.
February 10, 1846. n21y1

Fig. 6. Burr Higgins had his own freight forwarding business in addition to being manager of the railroad and head of the bank in Norwalk. He and his board borrowed money from their own bank which may have helped it to fail.

The road opened its entire length in June of 1846.... The cost of the road is stated at $702,111, machinery and cars $106,448 – total $808,560. Capitol stock, $450,000, indebtedness $387,385 – total $837,385. Available assets, $79,363.

	1846	1847
Earnings	$45,499	$85,403
Expenses	$17,437	$23,997
Net Receipts	$28,061	$61,406
Interest Payments	$17,704	$18,407
Passengers Carried	9873	20,737
Bushels of Wheat	360,256	504,081
Barrels of Flour	11,315	62,598

Burr Higgins suffered an embarrassing personal set back as reported in the *Sandusky Clarion* on February 20, 1847. The wheat warehouse, *belonging to B. Higgins & Co., at Paris (Plymouth) was broken down by the great weight of the wheat it contained, emptying it's contents onto the track, entirely obstructing traffic for the past week.*

Fortunately there were locomotives on both sides and passengers have met with very little inconvenience or delay.

Another set back occurred in June of 1847, when the steamboat *Chesapeake* sank after colliding with a schooner five miles from Conneaut. The old steamer was owned by the Mansfield and Sandusky City Railroad. The ships safe, containing between $8,000 and $9,000, went down along with the ships papers and passenger list. A story in the *Huron Reflector* said that an effort to raise the ships safe and engines would be made. There was no insurance, and many passengers that survived lost everything they had.

Before the line was even open to Mansfield a movement had been promoted to extend a railroad south to Newark. To the people in Licking County, who already had a canal, the realization came that rail transportation was much faster and could operate the year around. The canals were shut down in winter from December through April.

At a meeting held in Mansfield in December of 1845 General James Hedges was appointed chairman with William Patterson and Benjamin Johns as vice presidents. Burr Higgins and Benjamin McMahan were secretaries. The outcome of the meeting was the need to expand the as yet unfinished line from Mansfield south to the Ohio River by way of Zanesville to Marietta, or by New Philadelphia to Steubenville or Wheeling. A resolution was passed calling for, *the people of this section of Ohio will cordially unite all their exertions and energies for the construction of a railroad from Mansfield south-east by way of Loudenville, and the valley of the Mohican, to connect with the Baltimore and Ohio Rail-road at the Ohio River."*

This dovetailed with plans already underway in Newark for its first railroad called the *Columbus & Lake Erie*, which had been chartered on March 12, 1845. Voters in Licking County approved $100,000 in county funds, and stock sales proceeded well. A similar favorable vote for funds in Knox County allowed construction north to begin in August of 1847. The fact that the M&SC had reached Mansfield no doubt spurred construction, which began on both ends of the line.

Chapter 4

The March South

The April 30, 1850, edition of *Ohio Times*, a Mt. Vernon newspaper, reprinted an article that originally appeared in the *Newark Gazette*. It gives a report on the progress of building the railroad between Mansfield and Newark that is to be found nowhere else:

> *We stated last week that a beginning had been made laying down the iron from Mansfield to Bellville. The Engineer is busily engaged with a competent force in putting the finishing strokes on this portion of the road - 14 miles in extent - and no energies or means will be spared to have so much of the road completed and cars running over it by the 15th of May next.*
>
> *We are further assured on the best authority, that the Directors have made arrangements for the speedy completion of the entire route. Between Mt. Vernon and Newark the road is graded, necessary timber delivered, and all the work that can safely be done before the work of ironing actually begun, is done. Between Mt. Vernon and Bellville there is nothing lacking but a portion of timber, and that will certainly be ready in time unless there should be a failure of water.*
>
> *The contracts made sometime since for the iron chairs and spikes have been filled, and enough of these articles for the entire line have already been delivered or are ready for delivery. The iron rails, as our readers know, were purchased last summer, and are now ready to be shipped by the first boats on the opening of the New York canals. Assurances have been received from the Company's agent in New York, that the iron will be put through with dispatch. It will be delivered at both ends of the road - at Bellville and Newark, in order that work of laying down may proceed rapidly from both points.*

Things did not progress as quickly as all had hoped. Perhaps the rails were slow in arriving or didn't go down as planned, but it would appear that bridges may have held things up a bit. Trestle bridges near St. Louisville, over the North Fork of the Licking River, and a bridge over Dry Creek near Mt. Vernon spanned long distances. Building the railroad from Sandusky south had been across flat land and prairie until Plymouth. From there south through Mansfield began rolling hills. South of Mansfield things were much different. The tracks were forced to follow streams through valleys along the Clear Fork of the Mohican River, which meant crossing and re-crossing the same streams and branch feeders with numerous bridges and culverts. The road snaked its way from Mansfield to south of Independence (Butler) before the landscape became more friendly. To this day Butler citizens claim to be the only town in Ohio that had a railroad enter from the west and leave by the west!

The *Sandusky Democratic Mirror*, in its October 30, 1849, edition reported, *that the portion of iron which Burr Higgins was so successful in purchasing in Europe for the railroad from Mansfield to Newark, is now en-route from New York. 1000 tons have been shipped and there are 2000 tons more being shipped as rapidly as possible. It is of the best quality, manufactured in Wales of superior T-rail pattern, heaviest ever brought west.*

To speed construction, and perhaps add a little PR, they loaded one of their locomotives onto a sailing ship in June of 1850, shipped it over to Cleveland, had it reloaded onto a canal boat and sent 176 miles down the Ohio Erie Canal to Newark. The *Richland*, a 15-ton, single drive engine, arrived in Newark where it took several days to raise the engine and tender with screw jacks to get it out of the boat and onto rails that had been installed along the canal at Second Street. A newspaper commented that, *this was that Newark might hear the "snorting of the iron horse" upon their end of the road as fast as tracks can be laid.* Engineer Derrick and fireman Burns took several days to assemble and get the engine under steam, during which time it was reported, *Every man and boy in town devoted time to taking in the wonder.*

A story in the *Mt. Vernon Democratic Banner* told that, *by the time the engine was ready to steam up, a half dozen short cars arrived and the railroad iron was beginning to be delivered by canal boats at the foot of Second Street. The iron was laid out through Second Street, the track being kept near the curb stone on the west side of the street. The construction train commenced making its trips and the road was gradually pushed out towards the north.*

In the mean time a small passenger car was added and people were allowed to take short excursions up the line at a modest fare. A house that earlier had been the *Cully Tavern*, under the sign of the Black Horse, was rented as Newark's first railroad station. Seven contractors worked from both ends of the roadbed and by September 16 miles of the road north from Newark was open through Vanatta, St. Louisville, and Utica, to southern Knox County.

That same month the Directors leased the Huron and Oxford Railroad. Little is known of this nine mile long line. It was chartered in February of 1846 and ran in a south-westerly direction from the port of Huron to Oxford Township where it connected with the M&SC at a point called Prout Station. Not much of a town existed until the connection, and evidence suggests that only a general store, post office, school house, and a small station were built. Andrew W. Prout was the Postmaster and Station Agent. The road must have been entirely a horse-powered line until it was leased. It had been built on the same gauge, perhaps by plan.

When the canal opened to Cleveland, and Sandusky had two railroads operational, traffic on the Milan Canal, and consequently Huron's docks, slowed to a trickle. The Huron and Oxford Railroad was an effort to get back into the game. Huron was at a standstill while its neighbor, 10 miles to the west, boomed. Huron had a deep harbor at the mouth of the Huron River, but little else. The canal traffic to Milan was about finished.

MANSFIELD AND SANDUSKY CITY RAIL-ROAD.

NEW ARRANGEMENT.
THROUGH TO BELLVILLE.

FROM and after this date the Express train will leave Sandusky at 8 o'clock A. M., Mansfield at 12 M., arriving at Bellville at half past 12. Returning, leave Bellville at half past 2 o'clock P. M., Mansfield half past 3, and arrive at Sandusky at 7 o'clock P. M., connecting with the evening line of first class steamers for Buffalo.

Passengers going south by this route can take stages at Bellville on arrival of the cars, for Mt. Vernon, Newark, Lancaster, Zanesville and Columbus, arriving at these towns the same day, reaching Columbus early in the evening, forming the quickest and cheapest route to any of the above places. Fourteen miles of the road (from Mansfield to Bellville) is laid with T rail, and forms part of the Columbus & Lake Erie Rail Road. The company expect to complete this road to Newark by the 1st of October next, 60 miles from Mansfield, and 116 miles from Sandusky. Sixteen miles from Newark, north, is already completed and carrying passengers.

J. R. ROBINSON, Sup't.
Sandusky, Aug. 21, 1850.

Fig. 7. The "Sandusky Register" advised of new travel arrangements for those going south.

An advertisement in the August 21, 1850, edition of the Sandusky paper announced that the road was open as far as Bellville. Travelers could take stage coaches from that point to Mt. Vernon, Newark, Lancaster, Zanesville and Columbus. The road did not open to Newark until the evening of January 6, 1851, when an engine and four cars arrived from Sandusky. It would have been a cold day, but a large crowd was on hand looking up Second Street when the shrill whistle was heard, different than the one on the *Richland*, which people had been used to. It was the Company's newest engine, the *Newark*, with a train of four cars that was coming around the bend and into a cheering mass of people.

The *Newark Advocate* had not been in favor of building the line. It complained that, *our countrymen are to apt to run everything into the ground....* *and are to ready to undertake gigantic public works without having the means* *to pay for them.* It didn't bother to report its progress or arrival of the first trains. As a result, the railroad didn't bother to advertise its new timetables in their paper.

The two newest engines on the railroad were the *Bellville*, and the previously mentioned *Newark*. With a 4-4-0 wheel arrangement they were larger and heavier than the earlier locomotives. The names selected were a good public relations effort.

The line was far from finished. In its February 1851 report to Mansfield and Sandusky City Railroad stockholders the Directors spoke of completion of the 60 mile extension from Mansfield to Newark but cautioned:

> *Many of the fixtures which are necessary to its operation, remain to be finished,* *- such as side tracks, turn tables, depot buildings, wood houses, &c., and the rails* *will require adjustment and leveling during the Spring. The managers having* *that work in charge, expect to place the line in good condition, as soon as weather* *admits, and when done, the Columbus and Lake Erie road may be regarded as* *among the most substantial works of its kind.*

> *The Stockholders are aware that under the date of June 1, 1848, the Mansfield* *and Sandusky City Railroad Company leased the Columbus and Lake Erie Rail-* *road, agreeing to pay 8 percent upon the cost of the said railway, said rental pay-* *able 1st May and 1st November annually. It is to be regretted that the cost of the* *railway under this lease, has not been agreed on between the two corporations,* *the President and Directors of the Columbus and Lake Erie Railroad Company,* *having been much engrossed with matters incident to opening the road.*

The President and Directors of the Columbus & Lake Erie leased their railroad to the Mansfield and Sandusky City Railroad for one dollar! The lease was for 10 years, and the M&SC was to pay an annual rent equal to 8% of the total cost of construction. The estimated final building cost was $1,000,000, or $16,666.66 per mile. The lease did not set well with some people, particularly in Knox County where some tax money had been subscribed. Three County Commissioners took the C & LE to court. The case for the County was argued by the law firm of H. B. Curtis & Scribner, which in a 27 page brief made this point: *The authority to make a* *connection was an authority to enter into an agreement by which the two roads* *might work the two roads together. It did not contemplate a merger - - that one* *road should entirely absorb the other, and for a series of years be its sole owner* *and controller.* The Commissioners lost the case. Attorney Israel Dille, President of the Columbus & Lake Erie Railroad must have been relieved.

Although the Columbus & Lake Erie built the road they had no equipment or loco-motives. Apparently no funds were available and evidence from a January 1847 newspaper story states this was the plan all along. Only M&SC engines and cars were to be used, which is somewhat surprising considering the financial situation the Company found themselves in during 1849.

The expected increase in passenger and freight business did not materialize and the wheat crop throughout the state was down by one third. Wheat was the biggest cash crop for farmers and its transportation to Sandusky was always viewed as a key source of income, whether it was shipped as wheat or flour. The farmers loss of income effected the merchandise market, and to some extent, the passenger business.

Another factor was a cholera epidemic that hit Sandusky in late June, July and early August of 1849. It has been estimated that over 400 people died from the disease in a little over two months time. An accurate figure will never be known. The town, with a population of 5,000, saw better than half, some accounts say 2/3, of its residents flee for other places where they were often not welcomed or turned away. Some never returned to Sandusky. Children became orphans, and business ground to a halt. It was difficult even to find laborers to dig graves as residents and unidentified immigrants were sometimes buried in common mass graves in what became known as the *Cholera Cemetery*. The very few passengers arriving by train went immediately on board waiting boats that left as soon as practical. Freight traffic ground to a halt.

At the onset of the epidemic the town had seven doctors. Two died, two left town, and the remaining three were worked to exhaustion. Late in July two doctors arrived from Cleveland and a few days later two more arrived from Mansfield. Other help came from Cincinnati. Sandusky, the key point on the M&S, was a place to be avoided. The editor of the July 26, 1849, issue of the *Daily Sanduskian* commented, *This shutting up and flying has a bad effect at home, and must be disastrous abroad. It creates unnecessary panic among those they leave, and we should think the deserters would be unwelcome visitors where they go.*

On the weekend of July 28 and 29 seventy people were buried. All but two had died of cholera. Most were buried in the *Cholera Cemetery*, and the wheels of the wagons of the dead were to be heard from morning till night. Fifty more had been buried earlier on Tuesday and Wednesday of that week. The *Daily Sanduskian* attempted to report on actual burials but had difficulty separating wild rumors from fact. Late July and early August was the peak season for the disease. The newspapers were filled with quack cures, from burning sulfur to exploding gunpowder in the streets to purify the air. One cure, due to a misprint, was outright poison. Sandusky was in a state of panic, as were other affected towns all along the coast.

GUNPOWDER vs. CHOLERA.

We have frequently seen statements of the efficacy of gunpowder explosions in checking the ravages of cholera. It was used in 1832 and 1833 in London, Paris, Trieste, Malta, and in other portions of Europe, as well as in some parts of this country. It has also been tried recently, with success, at Lexington, Kentucky. The beneficial results have, in all cases, been ascribed to the disturbance of the air by the concussion, and no one seems to have given any of the credit to the gases disengaged by the explosion. It seems to us, however, more natural to conclude that the purifying of the air of its unhealthy qualities is caused by some counteracting influence in the gases evolved in the explosion, than by a violent concussion, which might be produced by other means.

We have been led to this conclusion partly by the analogy, which no one can fail to see, between this remedy and the sulphur and carbon remedy recently made public in Chicago. Two of the ingredients of gunpowder are sulphur and carbon, and in its explosion there is an evolution of carbonic acid, carbonic oxide, sulphurous acid, and, of course, nitrogen. If sulphur and carbon are as effective as they are said to be by the advocates of the so-called Chicago remedy, why not attribute equal effect to them in the shape of their gases disengaged by the explosion of gunpowder? The suggestion is, we think, worth the consideration of men of science, and it may be worth while to enquire also whether the nitrogen from the gunpowder had any share in neutralizing the noxious qualities of the cholera atmosphere.

Philadelphia Bulletin.

Fig. 8. Newspapers carried numerous "quack" cures for cholera which struck Sandusky in 1849. At least one, due to a misprint, was poison.

The *Daily Sanduskian* reported on August 20, 1849, that:

We again hear the sound of the caulker's hammer and the sailors cheerful voice, as they re-rig the vessels laid up during the prevalence of the cholera. The rumbling of other wheels than the dead cart and other voices than those of lamentation, break upon our ear.

Travel upon the railroads, has vastly increased the past few days, cars and steamers come and go, freighted with heavy loads of merchandise for the prosecution of an active fall trade. Produce which was in store, has been mostly shipped abroad, and leaves the market bare. Wheat, however, may be quoted at 93 cents (per bushel) from teams and 95 cents for good on board. We hear of 1000 bushels of corn at 44 cents, although we hear that the best would command 48 cents on board. Flour - none in market, no activity in other articles.

The road, since it's inception in 1840, had never paid its stockholders a dividend. Continual demands for buildings, locomotives, cars and maintenance outstripped available income. In addition, the Railroads Annual Report for 1850 spells out another sad story:

Upon the opening of spring navigation, in March last, a large amount of business was pressed upon the road; the motive power was to limited for it's extent, and the road bed was in a state far from satisfactory, and past circumstances rendered it necessary to restrict expenditure as much as possible, with a view to reduce and keep within the bounds of the floating debt.

Under a combination of these adverse circumstances, by which the ability of the company to operate the road was circumscribed and crippled; the owners of nearly all the old capitol stock were induced to negotiate for it's sale, and after three months' investigation into the past history of the concern, and into it's future prospects, the purchase and sale was consummated to parties in Ohio, and in the city of New York, whose determination it was and is, to make it a first class road in every respect.

The stockholders took a loss. A new mortgage was created for $730,000 from Mechanics Bank in New York at 7 per cent interest, payable twice a year, the full amount due on July 1, 1860. That was a lot of money in 1850, probably enough to buy most of present day Wyandot County. The Wyandot Indians had been moved off their 12 square mile reservation, and the land was being sold for $10.00 an acre.

List of Articles transported North over the Mansfield and Sandusky City Railroad, in 1849 and 1850.

		1849.	1850.
Wheat,	bushels of 60 lbs.	292,506	481,745
Corn,	" " 56	2,431	46,703
Beans,	"	96	1,608
Flour,	barrels,	8,910	12,381
Pork and Beef,	"	5,921	5,196
High Wines and Whiskey,	"	1,637	6,236
Eggs,	"	582	1,218
Apples and Cranberries,	"	38	352
Seeds,	pounds,	1,655,207	980,005
Butter, Lard, and Tallow,	"	737,619	953,836
Ashes, Pot, &c.,	"	434,061	466,723
Dried Fruit,	"	559,417	291,579
Tobacco in hhds. and boxes,	"	183,259	144,004
Wool and Pelt,	"	624,040	557,308
Merchandise and Sundries,	"	598,456	780,000
Staves,	No.	53,000	384,000
Lumber,	feet,	158,692	39,488
Live Hogs,	No.	2,371	4,870
Oil Cake,	pounds,	36,894	37,691
Oats, Rye, and Barley,	bushels,		14,291
Nuts,	barrels,		477

Fig. 9a: the 1849 shipping list.

B.

List of Articles transported South over the Mansfield and Sandusky City Railroad, in 1849 and 1850.

			1849.	1850.
Merchandise,	. . .	pounds, . .	6,721,240	8,228,000
Pig Iron,	. . . .	" . . .	274,424	244,000
Stone Coal,	. . .	tons, . . .	30	17¼
Fish, .	. . . .	barrels, . .	1,691	1,658
Salt, .	. . . .	barrels, . .	11,408	10,742
Lime, .	. . . .	" . .	1,506	1,181
Shingles, .	. . .	M, . . .	966	1,122
Lumber,	. . .	feet, . . .	220,628	116,764
Shingle Bolts,	. . .	cords, . .	30	14
Railroad Iron and Spikes,	.	tons, . .		5,036
Plaster,	. . .	barrels, . .		438
Lath, .	. . . .	M, . . .		12
Lime, .	. . .	bushels, . .		7,265
Barley and Malt,	. .	" . .		1,808
Cedar Posts,	. . .	No. . .		355
Live Sheep,	. . .	" . .		176

Fig. 9b: the 1850 shipping list.

Chapter 5

The Mansfield and Sandusky City Railroad in 1851

The stockholders report dated February 28, 1851, gives a very complete description of the railroad, its assets, buildings, rolling stock, and future plans. It is rare to find such an early publication which lists all the officers and stockholders. Evidently it was expanded over the usual report to inform the new owners and investors of what they actually controlled. The following is taken, in part, from those pages:

At Sandusky—A large stone block, presenting a front of about 210 feet, in which is contained the treasurer's and superintendent's offices, two passenger rooms, passenger car depot, stalls for five locomotives, machine, car and blacksmith's shops.

These various divisions are in good condition and sufficiently commodious, although additional engine and car depots have become indispensable by reason of the great present and prospective increase of motive power of the road.

The machine shop contains all the necessary tools and apparatus for the repairs of engines and cars, and the other machinery of the road. It has one large lathe for turning locomotive driving wheels, one lathe for turning railroad axles, one small lathe, one small iron planing machine, two machines for cutting bolts, one small press drill, one press for pressing wheels into axles, five vices, one small hand lathe, and one lathe for turning patterns.

The car shop has two circular saws, one circular planing machine, one Woodward do., one upright saw for cutting tenons. All the above is operated by a steam engine, of 10 in. bore and 20 in. stroke, and a boiler, having 11-6 inch flues and 16 feet long.

The blacksmith's shop has 10 fires, nine of which are in daily operation.

Also, one merchandise warehouse, 250 feet long by 60 wide; capacity, 20,000 barrels rolling freight. This warehouse is placed on a durable dock, filled with stone and faced with heavy oak timber, extending into the bay 300 feet.

One wheat warehouse, 300 feet long, 60 feet wide, 3 ½ stories high in the center; with two trucks, eight elevators and two lines of conveyance, operated by a first class steam engine; will store 320,000 bushels of wheat and 20,000 barrels of rolling freight. This building is also placed on a substantial dock or wharf, 350 feet in length, and having the necessary wharf-age accommodations for steamboats and other vessels.

During the present winter extensive additions have been made to the docks of the company, by sinking cribs and filling them in such a way that almost double of the former wharf-age space. One small transportation office, standing apart from the other buildings is chiefly used by the freight agent at Sandusky and his assistants.

In addition to these buildings, measures are in progress to erect during the coming spring, a substantial stone edifice, of about 400 feet in length, in which will be contained the necessary space for passenger cars, for various offices of the company, and rooms for passengers, baggage &c. When this is completed, the present building will be converted into an engine house.

At the Slate Run Station, the company own a substantial boarding house for the workmen on the road, and a large and convenient wood house, 100 feet in length; also at Havana, Paris (Plymouth), Shelby and Springmill, wood houses varying from 50 to 110 feet long. At Centerville, Paris, and Springmill are durable and well furnished boarding houses. The company also own, at Paris Station (Plymouth), two warehouses, one which is placed over the track, and especially designed for wheat; capacity about 120,000 bushels.

At Mansfield, a large brick depot, in which is situated the necessary offices, passenger rooms, platforms &c., on one side of the track, running through the building, and on the other a spacious warehouse for rolling freight. Also a brick engine house containing four stalls, and a blacksmith's shop under the same roof.

The Company also owns a valuable tract of wood land of 447 acres, about 26 miles from Sandusky, through which the track passes. The timber on this land is not only rapidly increasing in value, but is of great convenience in being able, in some degree, to control prices of fuel and timber on the line, by the facility with which it can be procured, if necessary, from that source.

During the fall, two first class passenger cars, one second class, and two baggage and post office cars have been purchased, and are in daily use, making in all 5 passenger cars now owned by the Company. In addition to these, a contract has been made for the delivery of six additional first class passenger cars and three baggage cars, all to be completed and delivered from time to time until the 15th of June next.

The Company now own nine locomotives, all in good condition for business; one of these is a small engine, chiefly employed in transporting timber for repairs,

Capital Stock of the Mansfield and Sandusky City Railroad Company, appearing on Books at Sandusky, Dec. 31, 1850.

	Shares.	
Ebenezer Lane and Robert Farley, Trustees, &c.	540	$27,000
State of Ohio,	666$\frac{2}{3}$	33,333
George Armentrad,	4	200
Francis Ashten,	6	300
Michael Arter,	4	200
Henry Arter,	1	50
Thomas W. Bartley,	20	1,000
William Bushnell,	4	200
N. B. Hogg, survivor of T. Bouman & Co.,	12	600
H. Bolgart,	4	200
Anthony Bell,	1	50
Stephen Bolgart,	2	100
John Bostwick,	2	100
Levi Burgheser,	3	150
George Cocher,	1	50
Amos Cook,	2	100
John Charles,	2	100
James Cartess,	4	200
James Ferguson,	1	50
Joseph Hoover,	2	100
Wm. Hartipee,	1	50
Absalom Jolly,	1	50
George Lilly,	1	50
Elijah W. Lake.	2	100
Daniel Mitchell,	2	$100
Allen G. Miller,	10	500
Alex. McBride,	2	100
Mark McDermot,	1	50
Archibald McBride,	5	250
James McKee,	2	100
John H. Milliken,	2	100
Jona Petit,	2	100
John Patterson,	2	100
Charles Palmer,	1	50
James Renfrew,	5	250
John Palmer,	2	100
John R. Robinson,	40	2,000
Asher Riley,	10	500
Hugh McFall,	7	350
Samuel Medy,	1	50
Samuel McCully,	1	50
Jacob Osborne,	1	50
Joseph Newman,	5	250
Isaac Osborne,	2	100
Daniel J. Swiney,	4	200
Chas. T. Sherman,	3	150
William Shagle,	1	50
John Van Tilbry,	2	100
E. P. Sturges & Co.	20	1,000
Wm. Taggart,	2	100
Geo. W. Warring,	3	150
Robert Yeoman,	2	100
Andrew L. Grimes,	3	150
Samuel Henshaw & Son,	40	2,000
Benjamin Johns,	129	6,450
John Sherman,	26	1,300
James Patterson,	2	100
A. H. Newbold,	10	500
H. Tanner,	12	600
Ebenezer Lane,	35	1,750
Robert Bowland,	12	600
Heirs of Willson McBride,	5	250
Arch. McBride and Heirs of Willson McBride,	2	100
D. N. Barney & Co.,	587	29,350
A. M. Marshall,	19	950
C. F. Sherman,	85	4,350
American Exchange Bank,	100	5,000
Geo. W. Penny,	500	25,000
John P. Renzer and John G. Camp, Jr.,	677	33,850
Hubbard Colby,	6	$300
Matthias Day,	4	200
Henry Grove,	2	100
David Young,	5	250
On the Books at Sandusky,	3,687$\frac{67}{100}$	$184,383 33

SCRIP STOCK.

Gibson, Stockwell, & Co.	586$\frac{1}{5}$	29,310
Ketchum, Rogers & Bement,	586$\frac{1}{5}$	29,310
John R. Robinson,	586$\frac{1}{5}$	29,310
C. T. Sherman,	586$\frac{1}{5}$	29,310
D. N. Barney & Co.	574$\frac{4}{5}$	28,740
Alfred Seton,	195$\frac{3}{5}$	9,780
John Haggerty,	120	6,000
Sidney Brooks,	180	9,000
Theodore Dehon,	136$\frac{1}{5}$	6,810
Francis Skiddy,	30	1,500
John Whitehead,	120	6,000
Oliver Slate, Jr.,	195$\frac{3}{5}$	9,780
Henry Grinnell,	195$\frac{3}{5}$	9,780
	4,092$\frac{60}{100}$	$204,630

Stockholders of the Mansfield and Sandusky City Railroad Company on Books of Mechanics' Bank, New York.

	Shares.	
D. N. Barney,	286	$14,300 00
D. N. Barney & Co.	658	32,900 00
L. S. Beecher,	5	250 00
Sidney Brooks,	510	25,500 00
J. L. Bunce, Cas.	1,277	63,850 00
Theodore Dehon,	389	19,450 00
Henry Grinnell,	555	27,750 00
E. T. H. Gibson,	300	15,000 00
Gibson, Stockwell, & Co.	814	40,700 00
John Haggerty,	340	17,000 00
Ketchum, Rogers & Bement,	810	40,500 00
A. B. Neilson,	333	16,650 00
H. M. Pinto,	2	100 00
J. A. Pinto,	2	$100 00
Oliver Slate, Jr.	555	27,750 00
Alfred Seton,	555	27,750 00
Francis Skiddy,	85	4,250 00
Spofford, Tileston & Co.,	850	42,500 00
Sinclair Tousey,	160	8,000 00
Wm. Aug. White,	333	16,650 00
John Whitehead,	340	17,000 00
	9,159	$457,950 00
Shares in the hands of Company,	40$\frac{33}{100}$	2,016 67
Shares discharged on books at Sandusky, for registration on Mechanics' Bank Books, New York,	1,020$\frac{40}{100}$	51,020 00
Total Shares,	18,000	$900,000 00

E. Lane and R. Farley, Trustees, hold 5,200 shares, which were as security for $260,000, of the old bonds, all of which have been cancelled, except $27,000, as stated in the foregoing Report. Out of this stock is to be issued the above 4,092$\frac{3}{5}$ shares, and in addition to this, 1,100 shares have been subscribed for at par, and will be delivered and paid for as soon as the stock is returned by Trustees. The balance of 19 shares will be issued out of stock still in the hands of the Company.

Fig. 10 and 11. Stockholder List

sawing wood &c. In addition to these, a contract has been made with Messrs. Rogers, Ketchum & Grosvenor, of New Jersey, for seven first class engines, to be delivered at short intervals from the opening of navigation until the first of September next.

The number of freight cars on hand at the time of the new organization in September last, was as follows: 70 four-wheeled wheat cars, 46 four-wheeled cars for ordinary freight, and 19 eight-wheeled platform and box cars. Since the 15th of September last, the Company has made in its own shops, 12 eight-wheeled box cars, and is now turning out without difficulty, eight cars per month, having put up an extensive stone addition during the fall, to their car and blacksmith's shops. A contract has also been made for 25 eight-wheeled box cars, to be delivered at the rate of 10 per month, and materials are now provided and on hand in our own yard for making a large number of additional cars during the next season, besides those above stated. Of the old cars on hand, six are worn out and useless, and 23 will require repairs. This will leave a perfect number at one hundred and forty one.

Measures have also been taken and contracts are being performed for the delivery of cross ties and other timber which will be required for laying the new rail.

During the fall of 1850 the Company had ordered 1100 tons of iron "T"-rails to replace the strap rails on the original roadbed. The flat bars came loose at the joints and had a tendency to curl upward as the wheels rolled over them. Occasionally one would come up through the bottom of a car and were referred to as *snake heads* by passengers. Although no serious injuries are recorded, engine crews carried a hammer and spikes in case they had to stop and nail down loose iron before continuing.

Fig. 12. The "Independence", one of seven new engines purchased from Rogers, Ketchum & Grosvenor in 1851. Early engine crews consisted of an engineer, fireman, conductor, front and rear brake men, and a wood passer. Photo courtesy Ohio Historical Society.

By December of 1850 all but 100 tons of the new rail had been laid *at such points on the line as exhibited the most serious decay. A contract has been made for 3800 tons of rails (the estimated weight required to complete the road) on favorable terms, so as to ensure the completion of the work no later than 1st of September. Whilst the iron is being laid, the ability to transport passengers alike with merchandise must of necessity be lessened."*

The *Democratic Mirror* also reported; *that the portion of iron that B. Higgins Esq. was so successful in purchasing in Europe for the railroad from Mansfield to Newark is now en-route from New York. 1000 tons have already been shipped and there are 2000 tons more being shipped as rapidly as possible. It is the best quality, manufactured in Wales, of superior T-rail pattern, heaviest ever brought west.*

With the new financing and merger came a new board of directors. Higgins was out and J. G. Forbes became the new president and treasurer. Other officers were:

Fig. 13. The Mad River & Lake Erie engine "Berwick", was built by Rogers in 1853. It appeared to be nearly new and was photographed on the Sandusky waterfront. Note ship mast to the left. Photo courtesy Hayes Presidential Library.

John Robinson	Superintendent, Mansfield
Charles Sherman	Mansfield
U. Jimeson	Mansfield
A. M. Marshall	Sandusky
A. H. Barber	Sandusky
E. S. Flint	Sandusky
L.S. Beecher	Sandusky
M. Mickey	Shelby
Thomas Hogg	Master Machinist

Evidence suggests that Higgins was somewhat of a wheeler dealer. After he and his backers picked up the charter of the closed bank in Norwalk and reopened it, he apparently loaned himself and the railroad interests so much money that the institution ultimately collapsed.

The prospects for profitability in 1851 and beyond looked good on paper. The new road was projected to pick up much of Newark's canal traffic. It would be faster, cheaper, and prospects were that Knox County, with its rich agriculture, would produce heavy traffic. But there were unforeseen circumstances that would hinder that expectation.

In September of 1850, at the time when the south end of the road was only open from Newark to the northern border of Licking County, a notice appeared in the Newark and Mt. Vernon papers:

$200 REWARD WILL BE PAID,—for the apprehension of the person or persons who set fire to the railroad bridge near John Campbell's, in Washington Township.

For the apprehension of the person or persons who lifted or misplaced the rails on the railroad track near John Lee's farm in Newton Township.

For the apprehension of person or persons who obstructed the railroad by placing a stake in the road track and laying rails or timbers across the track in the town of St. Louisville, on or about the 28th day of August.

No doubt the trouble came from teamsters and drovers who were going to be put out of business once the line opened. It's possible there was some dissatisfaction with the amount of compensation received from land owners, just as had happened in Plymouth. Farmers in the vicinity of present day Butler and Ankneytown also reportedly battled with fists and clubs over the right of way. In any event, the culprits were never arrested and for a while the railroad had to hire watchmen to guard the bridges from Newark all the way to Bellville. How badly the bridge was damaged or whether it had to be replaced, is unknown. Once the road reopened things calmed down.

Two months earlier the bridge over the Huron River at Monroeville apparently caught fire from a passing train and was reportedly destroyed for a distance of 180 feet. The company's crews had it rebuilt and back in service in 36 hours!

Cleveland, which had enjoyed the benefits of the Ohio and Erie Canal that had been snatched from Sandusky, watched with envy as their rival with its two railroads grew rapidly and threatened to become the leading lake port. Not wanting to be outdone the Cleveland leaders began a southern railroad of their own. Called the Cleveland Columbus and Cincinnati Railroad, it would cross the M&SC someplace. After trying to find backers in Mansfield and Mt. Vernon, which already had railroads, it gave up and crossed at Shelby. The CCC was finished from Cleveland to Shelby in November of 1850. The question was whether this would be an asset to the M&SC, or take away some of its traffic?

Fig. 14. Sam Clark (front left) with his railroad grading crew. It was nearly all hand labor. Photo is believed to have been taken near Mt. Vernon. Photo courtesy Carl T. Winegardner.

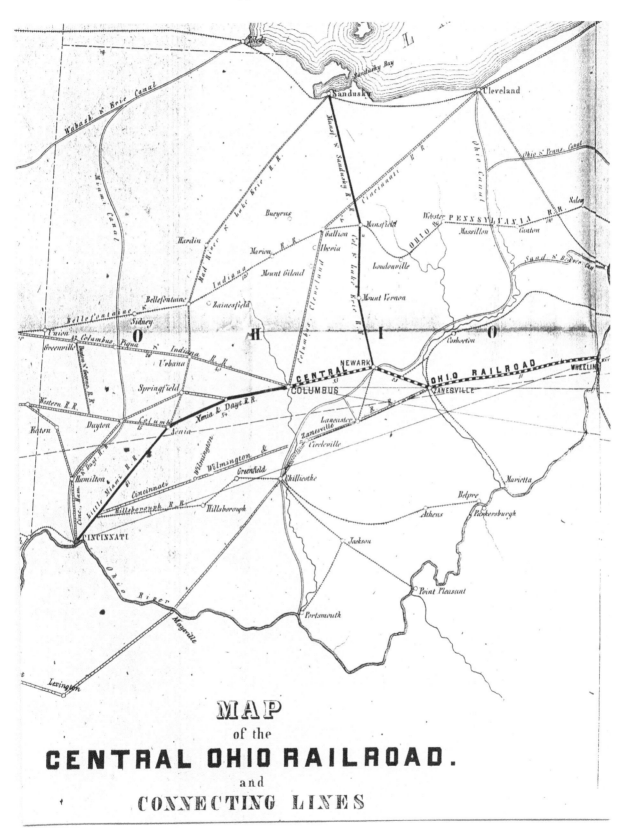

Fig. 15. An 1850 rail map of Ohio. Thin lines indicate proposed railroads or roads being built.

Chapter 6

The Challenges of the 50s

The total receipts from freight and passengers in 1850 amounted to $110,790.84. With the extension south completed, increased revenue was eagerly anticipated. The M&SC 1853 annual report is a study of the progress:

	1851	1852	1853
Freight	$166,655.12	$192,936.43	$177,896.72
Passengers	$67,977.66	$95,964.69	$136,544.58
Mail & Misc.	$6,349.47	$11,730.88	$10,972.30
Total	$240,982.25	$300,632.00	$325,423.60

The report mentioned that the drop in freight revenue in 1853 was due to the partial failure of the wheat crop. It was estimated that only 1/3 of the average crop had been produced, this reduced grain and flour shipments. The company always depended on shipments of these two items. A good portion of wheat was ground into flour and meal in the local water powered grist and flour mills. The abundant streams and fall of water courses created ample opportunities for mill sites. In

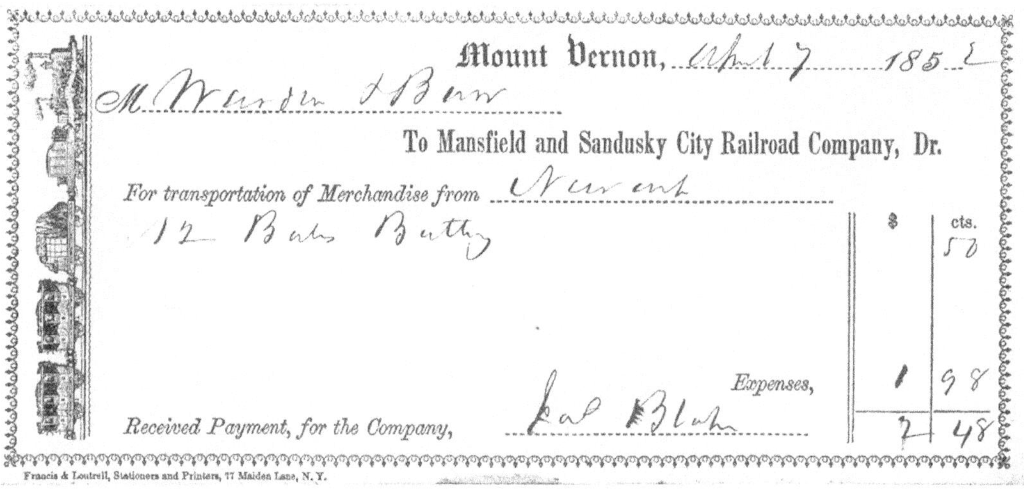
Mount Vernon, ... 185..

To Mansfield and Sandusky City Railroad Company, Dr.

For transportation of Merchandise from ....

	$	cts.
		50
Expenses,	1	98
Received Payment, for the Company,	2	48

Francis & Loutrell, Stationers and Printers, 77 Maiden Lane, N. Y.

Fig. 16. Freight Bill for the Sandusky, Mansfield and Newark Railroad. Courtesy of the Mark Hertzler Collection.

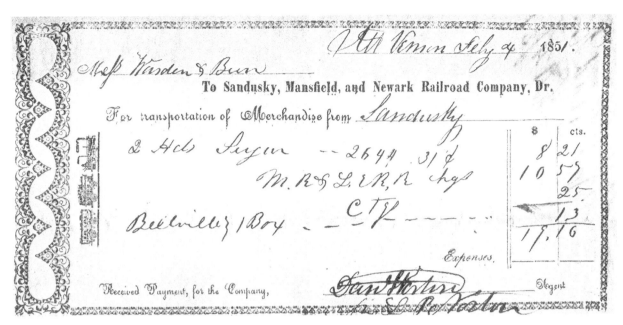

Fig. 17. Another Freight Bill for the Sandusky, Mansfield and Newark Railroad. Courtesy of the Mark Hertzler Collection.

1840, Richland County, the largest County in the state at that time, had 82 water powered gristmills and 106 sawmills, more than any county in the state.

By 1860 when it had been reduced in size by the creation of Ashland and Morrow Counties, it could still boast 34 water powered grist mills. Erie had 6, Huron 16, Knox 6, and Licking 28. The flour was shipped in wooden barrels, spawning another industry, barrel making. Only 12,000 barrels of flour were shipped in 1850. The amount would more than double over the next ten years. The peak year was 1849 when 62,598 barrels went north.

Railroading was not without its dangers. In March of 1851 a young man who was fixing some ropes on one of the freight cars was killed when he fell off and two of the car wheels ran over him. The accident happened near the depot in Mt. Vernon. The victim, John Sharrod, was from Mansfield. A month later, E. G. Stokes, conductor on the Empire freight train was killed at Plymouth. He was standing on top of one of the cars with his back to an oncoming bridge. The bridge knocked him off, breaking his neck, and he was run over by one of the cars.

Work was progressing on a road south from Newark. The Scioto and Hocking Valley Railroad was being built from Newark through Somerset and was to end at Portsmouth on the Ohio River. It was hoped that the 24 mile section to Somerset would be completed by the summer of 1854. This would take them into Perry County, one of the richest wheat producers in the state. The stockholders were told the region *will furnish an inexhaustible supply of Iron and Coal of the best qualities for the lake market. This crop has one valuable characteristic, - it never fails, and the demand is always in advance of the supply.*

Extensive docks were being built at Sandusky and Huron in anticipation of the new exports. The iron ore was found to be of poor quality but there was coal in those hills and plenty of it. All they had to do was get the rails to the right places. That, as it turned out, was to be a long time coming. The roadbed was graded, some bridges built, and a quantity of timber was on hand when the project went broke. It would lay that way for nearly 20 years until a coal company founded in Newark tried to finish it as far as Straitsville in Perry County. Then the coal company went broke and took a lot of investors with it. Newark however, would wind up with a source of cheap coal years later.

The M&SC sold two of its old locomotives to the Scioto and Hocking Valley in 1853. These were replaced by two, "heavy 10 wheel freight engines of 30 ton each, at a cost of $22,100. These engines are from the works of Rogers, Ketchum & Grosvenor, and are probably inferior to none in the country." These would have been the 4-6-0 *Mohican* and *Hocking*. Which old engines were sold is not mentioned. The oldest were the *Mansfield* (1844), the *Empire*, and *Vigilance* (1845). The *Vigilance* had the smallest cylinders and was the least powerful. It was once referred to as *a small engine, chiefly employed in transporting timber for repairs, sawing wood &c.* What happened to them after the unfinished S&HV went broke is unknown. It is possible that the M&SC got them back, or that they were shipped to Portsmouth for the partially finished southern end of the new road.

A list of 17 engines known to have been owned up until December 31, 1853 is as follows:

Mansfield	4-2-2?	10/44
Empire	4-4-0	7/45
Vigilance	2-2-0	7/45
Knox	4-2-0	6/46
Licking	4-2-0	10/46
Richland	4-2-0	4/47
Bellville	?	6/48
Newark	4-4-0	?/50
Plymouth	4-4-0	3/51

Lexington	4-4-0	3/51
Independence	4-4-0	4/51
Utica	4-4-0	4/51
Fredrick	4-4-0	8/51
Shelby	4-4-0	8/51
Sandusky	4-4-0	9/51
Mohican	4-6-0	7/53
Hocking	4-6-0	7/53

The Annual Report for 1853 states that the company had sold two old locomotives, bought two new ones to replace them, and had in running equipment 16 engines.

On May 10, 1853, the Sandusky paper reported a major wreck:

The freight train which left here at six-o'clock yesterday morning on the Sandusky, Mansfield and Newark Railroad, was thrown from the track near Lexington, by coming into contact with a cow. Being near a bridge which spans a small stream, the engine was precipitated into the water. We are pained to state that the Conductor, Mr. James Teegarden, of Mansfield, the Engineer, Joseph St. Peters, and the Fireman, named McLear, were instantly killed. The two latter were horribly mutilated. Mr. Teegarden, it is said, was thrown into the water, and when the dispatch was sent, his body was still under the ruins. The Engineer resided at Newark, and leaves a family. We have not learned of the probable amount of damage done to the train.

In September of 1854, another accident occurred just north of Independence (Butler), and was reported in the Mansfield *Shield & Banner*:

It appears that the Mail Train - Conductor Jackson - coming north was ahead of the freight train on its usual time, and stopped to wood. The "Hocking" freight train, - James Hays engineer- having disregarding the rules as to fast running, and passing the station at Independence without stopping, - another violation of the rules - came up at full speed and struck the hinder most passenger car which had quite a number of passengers in it, splitting it entirely in two, injuring more or less most of the people in it....The whole blame is attached to the engineer of the "Hocking," who was promptly discharged by the vigilant and watchful superintendent of the road, Mr. J. R. Robinson.

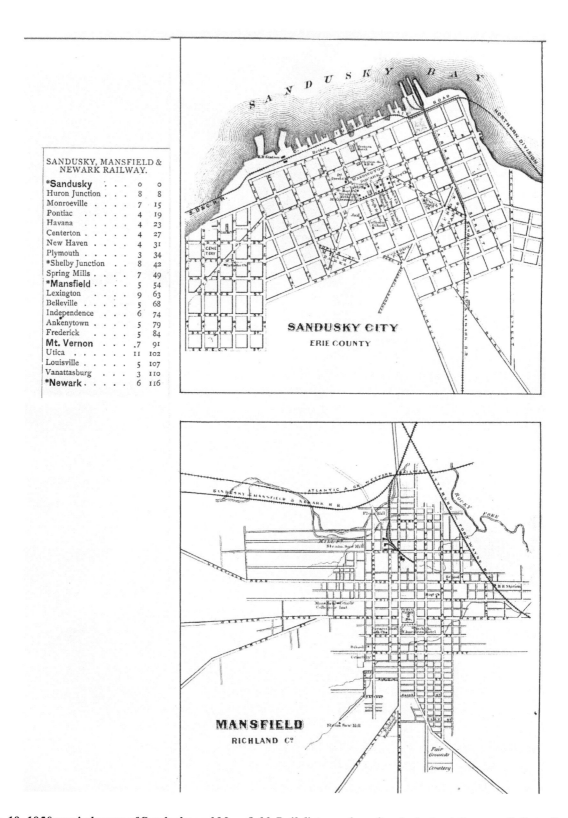

SANDUSKY, MANSFIELD & NEWARK RAILWAY.		
*Sandusky	o	o
Huron Junction	8	8
Monroeville	7	15
Pontiac	4	19
Havana	4	23
Centerton	4	27
New Haven	4	31
Plymouth	3	34
*Shelby Junction	8	42
Spring Mills	7	49
*Mansfield	5	54
Lexington	9	63
Belleville	5	68
Independence	6	74
Ankenytown	5	79
Frederick	5	84
Mt. Vernon	.7	91
Utica	11	102
Louisville	5	107
Vanattasburg	3	110
*Newark	6	116

SANDUSKY CITY
ERIE COUNTY

MANSFIELD
RICHLAND C?

Fig. 18. 1850s period maps of Sandusky and Mansfield. Rail distance from Sandusky to stations south lists all stops on the line.

Chapter 7

Consolidation and a New Company

A dividend of 4% had been paid to the stockholders in July of 1853. It was the first one ever paid. As expenses and competition increased, it was to be the only one! On December 29, 1853 the three companies, Huron & Oxford, Mansfield and Sandusky City, and the Columbus and Lake Erie Railroads were merged into one consolidated corporation named the Sandusky Mansfield & Newark Railroad. The 127 mile road had a combined debt in stock and bonds of $3,552,357.40! Or, about $28,000 per mile.

The consolidation didn't work. The road continued to sink deeper in debt with creditors who finally filed a suit in Erie County. A meeting was held by the Bond-holders and Stock-holders at the Astor House in New York City on July 10, 1855. Their plan of adjustment of the financial difficulties involved several actions. First, all holders of bonds relinquish two years interest for 1855 - 56. The old bonds were to be replaced by new 7% bonds secured by a new mortgage. All unpaid taxes, claims for labor and material, and past due original bonds were to be paid out of the earnings of the road. It was also directed, *That a receiver be appointed in the case now pending in Erie County, Ohio, with full power to take possession of and manage the entire road ....to appoint and remove all the officers, servants, and employees, other than the President and Directors.* This plan somehow was supposed to reduce the debt of the company from about $4,000,000 to a new limit of $2,400,000. John R. Robinson of Mansfield was appointed manager.

At that time the SM&N had the following equipment;

Eight 8-wheel Locomotives,	1st class
Two 10-wheel Locomotives,	1st class
Two 8-wheel Locomotives,	2nd class
Three 6-wheel Locomotives,	3rd class
Twenty 8-Wheel Stock Cars	

Forty Gravel Cars

Thirty Hand Cars

Nine First Class Passenger Cars

Three 2nd Class Passenger Cars

Six Mail and Baggage Cars

137, 8-Wheel Box Cars

76, 8-Wheel Platform Cars

Twenty Ditching Cars

Things didn't get better under the receivership. A year later the bankrupt road was sold by a decree of the Erie County Court. The stockholders took a big loss and the road was again re-organized and secured under a single mortgage of $1,290,000 on July 25, 1856.

The August 13, 1856 edition of the "Newark Advocate" summarized the situation:

The new company starts with a clean balance sheet, and is fortunate in having passed through an ordeal which it would appear is to be the fate of many embarrassed Railroads. The theory of compromising the affairs of these monster corporations, so that all parties may have something of value, and come in on some equitable scaling of securities, is obtaining favor, and we think will be generally adopted.

This was the pioneer case of the kind, and in its progress has brought out some of the very ablest counsel in the country.

H. H. Hunter, of Lancaster, was counsel for the corporation, and to his eminent judicious advice and direction, the parties are greatly indebted for the result. The agents for carrying out the arrangement by procuring the signatures of the parties in Ohio, viz: Messrs. Wright, of Newark; Woodward, of Mt. Vernon: Camp, of Sandusky; in connection with Mr. Gibson, of New York, have accomplished a great work, and we trust are amply rewarded by the results.

The roadbed was in poor condition. Many of the bridges and nearly all the trestle work along the line were in a state of dilapidation and decay. It was deemed unsafe to pass over some of them. Many of the cross ties were decayed and rotten as few had been replaced since the line was built. The rebuilding of two bridges near St. Louisville at the southern end of the line, was the only big undertaking. The treasury was empty and employees and expenses went unpaid for months. Robinson was gone and John R. Webb, who had originally been employed as an engineer in locating the path of the road, took over as new Superintendent.

Earnings had been decreasing since 1854. The opening of the Ohio & Pennsylvania Railroad, and the Pittsburg Ft. Wayne and Chicago Railroad, through Mansfield, and the Central Ohio line from Columbus, through Newark to Zanesville, each took a toll. The Cleveland Columbus and Cincinnati passed through Shelby. Each of these lines was on a different gauge than the SM&N. Their cars would not interchange. The SM&N had lost its credit and the wheat crop was down again, possibly due to weather and poor farming practices. The SM&N always pegged their freight hopes on the wheat crop.

John Webb took his new post seriously. In his first 13 months on the job, December 1st of 1855 to December 31st 1856, he walked the entire track from Sandusky to Newark. He noted the poor dilapidated conditions and went to work on reconstruction. Part of his first report is as follows:

> The two old trestle bridges over "North Fork of The Licking" near St. Louisville, 542 feet long, have been rebuilt, with abutments and piers of stone in place of the temporary supports, consisting of 377 cubic yards of first class masonry 296 lineal feet of bridging on "Howe's improved plan," by Messrs. Thatcher, Burt & Co., and 246 feet filled with 2500 cubic yards of earth work by R. Durbin.

> The old bridge over "Dry Creek" near Mt. Vernon, 410 long, has been reconstructed by 360 cubic yards of masonry in abutments, one span of 120 feet of "Howe's Patent truss bridge," and 290 feet filled with 4,171 cubic yards of earth work. The bridge over "Vernon River," formerly 356 feet long, has been rebuilt with 480 cubic yards of masonry, two spans of 120 feet each of "Howe's patent bridge," and 116 feet filled with 1200 cubic yards of embankment.

> The old bridge over "Lick Run," south of Centerville, (Centerton) 396 feet long, has been filled with 5,100 cubic yards of embankment, and an arched culvert of 20 feet chord has been constructed, requiring 115 cubic yards of first class masonry. The "Big Slate Run" bridge near Pontiac, 910 feet long, has been reconstructed the erection of an one span bridge of 108 feet in length, of "Howe's Truss," with stone abutments containing 259 cubic yards of masonry, and the balance (802 feet) has been filled with earth, consisting of 20,150 cubic yards of embankment. The bridge over "Fink Run," two miles south of Monroeville, 600 feet long, has been filled with earth, requiring 5,000 cubic yards - - the stone work having been completed by my predecessor.

> Thus the whole 3,700 feet of old "trestle bridging," whose average height was at least 20 feet, has been rebuilt without interruption to the running of train for a single day.

The editor of the *Newark Advocate* commented in the December 17, 1856 issue:

The new bridge over Dry Creek, is a very fine structure, with a span of over one hundred feet. It was an institution much needed a fixture there heretofore,with its rotten abutments, being wonderfully suggestive of the valley and shadow of death. The idea of constructing a bridge of such dimensions on a rail line that is daily occupied by passenger and freight trains would be too preposterously absurd to cipher out, but in this fast age, impossible is swept from the vocabulary and wonders spring up every day.

In addition to the bridge work, Webb and his crews installed 40,000 new cross ties and noted that 40,000 or 50,000 more would be needed in the coming year. Several more bridges would need to be rebuilt. The weather took its toll on the native timber used.

The rolling stock included:

> 2 ten-wheel engines of 30 ton each
>
> 5 eight-wheel engines of 23 tons each
>
> 3 eight-wheel engines of 20 tons each
>
> 2 single-driver engines if 15 tons each
>
> 1 single-driver engine of 9 tons

The engines are all in good working order except two or three which have been laid up for temporary repairs; five new flue sheets have been put into them, and new sets of tyre have been put onto four during the past year at a cost, I am informed by Mr. Hogg, the Master Machinist, of not less than $3,500 over and above ordinary repairs.

The road was in much better shape in 1857 due to the efforts of Mr. Webb, but it wasn't to be a banner year by any means. Gross receipts were down 27.5% from 1856, $215,114 versus $296,949. The opening of what was then called the Pittsburgh Ft. Wayne and Chicago Railroad through Mansfield had taken a large part of their freight and passenger business. This they could not hope to recover. The Directors came to the realization that they were operating a North - South line and could not expect the "through" business they had hoped for. The roads business would have to be regarded as "local" in nature.

There were other problems. The President, William Key Bond, resigned. They would be unable to make bond payments on time. The huge Freight Warehouse at Sandusky burned down, and the locomotive *Frederick* blew up. Outside of that things didn't look to bad!

On October 2, 1857, the steam propeller *Republic* left the railroad's dock and headed out of the harbor only to discover storm tossed high waves. She returned to the dock, tied up on the east side of the rolling freight warehouse and the captain decided to lay over until the next day. Everyone left the fully loaded boat. At about 3:30 in the afternoon a fire was discovered on board.

The three Sandusky fire companies were sent for and attacked the burning boat. Ogontz Company No.1 (Ogontz was the original name for Sandusky) drug their heavy hand pump engine and hose reel through the warehouse to the north end of the dock with the plan to attack the fire from there. As they were setting up the Republic burst into a huge ball of fire which, with the wind, set the warehouse on fire. The trapped firemen had to escape the burning dock by boat and watch help-lessly as Sandusky's newest, and largest, piece of fire equipment was destroyed. Within thirty minutes of discovery the upper deck of the Republic and the ware-house were in ruins.

The fun wasn't over yet. A newspaper account in the *Sandusky Register* tells the story best:

> *Mean time the wooden locomotive house, to the right of the warehouse, had also ignited, and for a time the prospect for saving it seemed dismal. A number of the largest and most valuable locomotives of the railroad company were inside. Ropes were attached to these and by great exertions they were pulled out and placed on track behind Water Street. The engines (two remaining hand powered fire pumps) also commenced playing on the building, lines were formed for the passage of water up ladders to the roof and after an hour of superhuman conten-tion with the fire, it was extinguished.*

> *By this time, the destruction of the warehouse being complete, the firemen turned their attention to the blackened hull of the propeller, from which steady burning continued. A few minutes after five o'clock, a change of the wind sent the burn-ing hull rapidly around, bringing it along side the open shed salt house of the railroad company, and its blazing stern within a few feet of the company's large grain warehouse on the opposite dock. The scene was now exciting in the extreme. The imminent danger to this second warehouse, as well as to the salt house and a number of cars standing on the track inside, was holding the immense crowd almost breathless. A schooner was also lying against the dock of the grain ware-house, but by means of lines, she was quickly jerked out of danger. The salt house took fire at once and the cars were quickly drawn out and run up on side tracks. One of the two engines remaining in use commenced throwing water on it and succeeded in holding the flames in check. The efforts of the other engine, with those of the crowd as did any work, were turned toward saving the large grain warehouse, which, not withstanding a wind from the propeller dead against it,*

S. M. & N. R. R.

CHANGE OF TIME.

TO TAKE EFFECT MONDAY, JULY 13, 1857.

| GOING SOUTH. | | | GOING NORTH. | |
| LEAVE. | | STATIONS. | ARRIVE. | |
Mail.	Accom'n.		Mail.	Accom'n.
6:35 A M	8:00 A M	Sandusky.	5:50 P M	4:00 P M.
7:21	9:25	Monroeville.	5:10	2:35
7:58	10:30	Centerville.	4:40	1:30
8:23	11:10	Plymouth.	4:20	12:50
8:52	12:00 M.	Shelby Junc	3:57	12:05
9:22	1:05 P M	Mansfield "	3:30	10:45 A M
9:47	2:20	Lexington	3:07	9:40
10:05	2:45	Belleville.	2:52	9:10
10:20	3:20	Independ'ce.	2:40	8:45
10:55	4:25	Frederick.	2:12	7:45
11:15	5:00	Mt. Vernon.	1:58	7:10
11:53	6:05	Utica.	1:28	6:05
12:30 P M.	7:00 ar.	Newark.	1:00 leave	6:00 le're

J W. WEBB, Supt.

Mad River & Lake Erie R. R.

CHANGE OF TIME.

ON and after Monday, July 13, and until further notice Passenger Trains will run daily (Sundays excepted) as follows :

GOING SOUTH.

LEAVE HUNTSVILLE.	DAY EXP.	MAIL.	NIGHT EXP.
Sandusky.....	7:30 A.M	11:30A.M.	8:30 P.M.
Clyde.........	8:10	12:20	9:20
Tiffin	8:50	1:00	10:04
Carey	9:30	1:40	10:55
Forest.......	9:56	2:20	11:35
Kenton......	10:20	2:48	12:05
Huntsville...4:45 A M	10:58	3:26	1:15
Bellefontaine 5:05	11:10	3:38	1:30
West Liberty 5:25	11:30	4:00	1:50
Urbana......6:50	12:00	4:25	2:20
Springfield ..6:35	12:36	5:08	3:05
Reach Dayt'n 7:50	1:30	6:12	4:40

GOING NORTH.

LEAVE	MAIL.	CLEV. EXP.	HUNTSVILLE.	NIGHT EX.
Dayton......11:40 A.M.	8:00 A.M.	6:25 PM	10:50 P.M.
Springfield ..12:36	8:50	7:40	11:44
Urbana 1:20	9:18	8:20	1:214
West Liberty 1:46	9:38	8:40	12:35
Bellefontaine 2:08	9:58	9:10	1:00
Huntsville... 2:20	10:08	9:25	1:15
Kenton 3:02	10:42		2:08
Forest 3:33	11:15		2:42
Carey ... 4:04	11:50		3:10

Fig. 19. Newspapers carried railroad timetables and advertising for lake shipping firms. This enlarged copy is from an 1857 Sandusky Register.

they succeeded in doing. Between six and seven o'clock the wind changed again, swinging the propeller back to its original position.

The Republic's cargo had consisted of 286 barrels of flour and live cattle and hogs. At the SM&N dock she took on board another 250 barrels of beer, 62 barrels of eggs, 57 kegs of butter, along with other items. The boat was owned by the New York & Lake Erie Railroad Line and was insured for $14,000. It burned to the water line.

The SM&N Warehouse losses were, among other things, 15 tons of merchandise recently landed and due to be delivered south along the line, 250 sacks of salt, 3 safes and 1 piano forte. The warehouse was only insured for $5,000, which would not be enough to cover replacement. It's probably just as well the piano burned up. It's doubtful anybody felt like singing.

On December 24, 1857 the engine *Frederick* exploded about a quarter mile from Monroeville. It had waited about half an hour for a Cleveland & Toledo train to cross where their tracks intersected, and had just left the station when the blast occurred. The boiler blew into pieces, some of which were found 40 to 80 rods away. Fences on both sides of the track were laid flat and 200 pound chunks of metal stripped through trees. Fragments of the bell were found 120 rods away in a field. A reporter described the scene; *The flues of the boiler were twisted into an almost solid mass, the heavy cylinders twitched off, battered, carrying with them the pistons and part of the connecting rods. The truck and driving wheels, with heavy spokes of solid wrought iron, were bent wholly out of shape; - in short, the engine was blown to fragments, an utter wreck beyond the possibility of repair.*

The engineer and fireman were blown back into the tender and by some miracle survived. The fireman suffered a bad cut on his head and a few scalds, but his partner, slightly scalded, fared better. The engines boiler had recently been rebuilt with new bottom sheets and was supposed to be as good as new. Whether the culprit was low water, cold water being injected to quickly, or metal failure, was not determined. When the venerable Englishman Thomas Hogg, Master of Machinery, arrived at the scene on another train his broad English salutation to the engineer was, *Aye, William, where was your wather?* As he drew closer, hearing no answer, he again asked, *Aye, William, where was your wather?* If there was an answer the reporter didn't record it. The *Frederick* had cost $8,500 new in 1851 and was valued at $5,000 when it blew up.

John Webb's report to the stockholders listed the rolling equipment and commented *that the three single driver engines are but of little value or use to the Company, except to run on the "Huron Branch." The balance are in good working* *order, with the exception of the locomotive "Jerry Myers," which is estimated by the Master Machinist, to cost $1,500 to put in running order.*

This engine may have been purchased used or from some other line, possibly in the east. It was the only engine to carry a person's name rather than a village, city or county as had all the others. Who was Jerry Myers? No one by that name was a board member or major stockholder. No other information has been found as to type or builder. The SM&N five-foot-four-inch gauge was unlike any other connecting road which may account for the large expense. The April 24, 1854, edition of the *Mt. Vernon Democratic Banner* carried a story about the firm of Cooper & Clark in which that company had a contract to build a locomotive for the Scioto & Hocking Valley Railroad. If they did, and the road went broke before rails were laid, perhaps the SM&N bought it. Cooper & Clark were also supposed to build four more for the SM&N in 1854, but that order was either canceled or never filled. Both roads were on the same gauge. This was to be the only mention of that engine.

Cooper & Clark made good stationary and portable steam engines in the early 1850s. Their locomotives were claimed to be the first ever built west of the Alleghenies. The Mt. Vernon firm faced one handicap in attempting to succeed in the railroad business. The SM&N was on the damnable five foot four inch gauge, making it extremely difficult to deliver completed engines

Commercial Affairs.

Sandusky Market.

SANDUSKY, August 7.

New wheat begins to come forward, though the arrivals as yet are small. There is considerable offering, to be delivered within 10 or 15 days. The best white samples at present sell at $1 20@ 1 25 on track. Red ranges at $1@1 15. Sales 400 bu Red and a small lot of white. Buyers are rather cautious and not disposed to make heavy purchases at present rates, anticipating a decline soon as the new crop is in market. Farmers who sell immediately will undoubtedly realize the highest prices.

FLOUR—Dull and but little doing. Small sales at $6 50 for good brands. Supply limited.

CORN—On track 68c. Arrivals fair.

OATS—Few coming forward per R. R.; 50c on track.

SALT—$1 60 ℔ bbl by the car load.

FISH—Quotations unchanged. Market inactive.

POTATOES—Dull. Market well supplied at 50c; prices declining.

EGGS—10c and more plenty.

BUTTER—16c and in fair request.

LARD—13@13½c.

WHISKY—25c.

[TELEGRAPHED EXPRESSLY FOR THE COM. REGISTER.]

New York Market.

NEW YORK, August 7.

FLOUR—Buoyant. Sales 6000 bbls at $6 30@6 50 for super State; $6 70@6 80 for extra State; $6 30 @6 50 for super Western; $6 65@7 for extra do; Canadian $6 40@6 50 for super; $6 75@8 75 for extra do.

WHEAT—Scarce and in request at better prices. Sales 7000 bu at $1 85 for prime white Canadian; $1 42 for inferior Mil Club.

RYE—Lower and dull; $1@1 05.

Fig 20. Market reports were closely watched by farmers and dealers. (August 1857)

on the SM&N to railroads of the standard four-foot-ten *Ohio* gauge. A small notice in the July 25, 1854, *Mt. Vernon Democratic Banner* relates; *One of Coopers fine locomotives has recently been purchased by the Central Ohio Railroad Company, and is now performing good service on that road. Messrs. Cooper & Clark have at the present two locomotives "on stocks," and will have them completed in the leaves of the fall.*

The engine *G. T. Clark* was delivered to the Central Ohio in July of 1854, and the *Licking* in October. Both were listed as 28-ton engines. The railroad was unable to pay for the engines ($8,750 each) and other equipment according to terms, and after four years Charley Cooper took them to court in what became a bitter, nasty, contest during which time Cooper attempted to seize the railroads property and tied up the roads bank assets. In Licking County District Court Cooper and Clark claimed they had sold the Central Ohio, *equipment's and machinery in the amount of $25,000 and a portion of this indebtedness had been transferred to other parties.* A settlement was finally reached with the nearly bankrupt railroad, but this may have turned Cooper & Clark against the railroad locomotive business. A descendent of the firm (Cooper Energy, now owned by Rolls Royce) still has a presence in Mt. Vernon and is one of its oldest manufactures. A beautiful color rendition of the first Cooper & Clark engine is on display at the Knox County Museum in Mt. Vernon.

The only bridge replaced in 1857 was over the *Vernon River* two miles north of Mt. Vernon. The 332-foot-long trestle was replaced with earthwork and a 120 span of *Howe's Truss* at a cost of $4,000.

John Webb left the SM&N on April 1, 1858, to take receivership of the Scioto & Hocking Valley Railroad. His successor, William Durbin from Sandusky was *baptized* twelve days later when a flood washed out the double bridge over the *Vernon River.* Both 130-foot spans and the center masonry pier were washed away. The bridge had been in use only 15 months and was a severe loss to the company. Contracts were let to replace this and other large bridges which were in bad shape.

The Company's Merchandise Warehouse and the wharf on which it stood had burned to the water line. A new dock, filled with 50,000 cubic feet of stone, was raised four feet above the lake level, and a new warehouse 200 by 76 feet was built, *conveniently arranged and covered with a superior tin roof.* The Grain Warehouse on the next dock had been built three feet above the lake level, but during 1857 the lake had risen four feet, submerging the grain receiving vaults and making it necessary to raise them eighteen inches. Its dock also had decayed and needed rebuilding.

The 1858 Report added; *The locomotive house at Sandusky has been entirely rebuilt, and of enlarged dimensions; it is now a very convenient and substantial structure, covered with tin and as far as practical, rendered fire-proof. The tracks in and about the yard have been remodeled to increase our car-stowage materially. The engine house and turn table at Newark have likewise been fitted up. A breakwater has been built at Huron to protect our buildings at that place.*

In addition, the water stations at Sandusky, Huron Junction (Prout), Monroeville, Pontiac, Plymouth, and Newark were repaired and new tanks added with an aggregate capacity of 25,000 gallons. Nearly 50,000 cross ties (about 400 per mile average) were used. Many of the wooden freight cars had suffered the ravages of the weather and needed repair. Although not a profitable year due to reconstruction costs, it was an improvement to previous years. *The policy of permitting the capitol to depreciate, that the apparent profits may be swelled, is deemed unwise, if not dishonest.* This policy would continue into the future.

Chapter 8

Into The 60s

On April 9th and 10th of 1860, an *extraordinary freshet*, the railroad's description of a flood, hit the southern portion of the road. It materially damaged or swept away 16 of their bridges or culverts.

There were two factors that account for these losses. First, timber was being stripped from the land at an alarming rate. The railroad alone accounted for much of this, and the demands on the forests' for new buildings, firewood, fencing, barrel making, and export shipments of lumber (27,026 ft. of black walnut in 1846). Compounding the problem this left bare lands that once held back rain water. In 10 months time in 1858 the road carried 2,161,425 feet of lumber, 4,823,842 M shingles and lath, and 300 car loads of barrel staves! It also purchased about 6,000 cords of wood for fuel, and was using nearly 40,000 cross ties per year.

Secondly, poor farming practices led to rapid runoff and soil erosion. Crop rotation and contour farming would not come into practice until years later when much of what was premium farm land had been ruined.

For its part, the railroad had narrowed some stream beds when building bridges. Replacing trestles with earthen embankments created a dam like effect during periods of flooding. It appears doubtful that engineers understood or appreciated that each new year would see higher water than in previous floods.

A new Truss Bridge with a 140-foot span was built over the North Fork of the Licking River to replace one swept away. A new bridge with a larger water way, 203 feet long, was built over Owl Creek half a mile north of Fredericktown. Another bridge, 186 feet in length, was built over the Clear Fork of the Mohican on the north side of Lexington, and an embankment replaced 207 feet of trestle at that place. The total amount of bridging built in 1860 was 1172 feet.

A new side track 400 feet long was built near the *summit* between Mansfield and Lexington. This was the highest point of elevation between Newark and

Fig. 21. The Alta, or Summit Station as it was earlier called, was the highest point on the SM&N between Newark and Sandusky. Photo about 1909

Sandusky. It would take on the name *Summit Siding*, and in later years *Alta*. It was used for car storage and trains to pass. A *Y* for turning cars and engines was added in later years. The track between south bridge at Mt. Vernon and Utica (10 ¼ miles) was rebuilt and ballasted with gravel, 44,442 cross ties were replaced on the main line and sidings during the year, and new water tanks built at Mt. Vernon and Utica. A new $750 turntable was built at Sandusky along with a 45 by 170 foot long shelter capable of holding nine passenger cars on three tracks for passengers and baggage.

It was reported that, *Three of our locomotives, the "Hocking," "Licking," & "Lexington," have been remodeled and thoroughly rebuilt during the last year....Five other engines are in fair running order and requiring but unimportant repairs to maintain their efficiency. Two others will require rebuilding this year.*

Total receipts had exceeded operating expenses by $34,000 for the year but this was still not enough to pay all the past due bond and mortgage expenses. However, things were looking better.

1861 would see a drop in revenue. Fortunately a decrease in operating expenses more than offset this. The company finished the year with a $37,610 surplus that would go to past due payments. The Company wasn't out of the woods, but it wasn't sinking deeper in debt either.

Bridge replacements, nine of them in 1861, for a total length of 1369 feet, were mostly in the Lexington, Bellville, and Butler area.

These were a heavy drain on the budget. James H. Stewart, the Assistant Superintendent of the road, wrote in his 1861 report to the stockholders:

> *Seven and one half miles of road between Plymouth and Monroeville have been thoroughly graveled, and the most part of the track rebuilt. A new side track at Hunt's Mill, 400 feet in length, has been built with mostly defective T. Rail. Side tracks at Newark, Mt. Vernon and Independence, have been improved by using 2000 feet of the defective T. Rail, in place of the Strap Rail tracks, which had become worthless. There is now on hand 51 tons of T. Rail which cannot be repaired. We also have 47 tons of Strap Rail not in use.*
>
> *The turn table at Mansfield has been rebuilt, the Engine House, tracks, and platforms at the Freight House have been thoroughly repaired. The track for the turn table at Huron has been rebuilt, and the Turn Table, Engine House, tracks and Grain House, have been repaired. The masonry and bents to the bridges along the Road, have been well protected with heavy boulders, and will now withstand any ordinary flood.*
>
> *The number of cars built during the year is as follows;*
>
> | | |
> |---|---|
> | *1 Baggage car* | *6 Platform Cars* |
> | *4 Hand cars* | *6 Dump or Ditching Cars* |
> | *5 Box or Grain Cars* | |
>
> *The number of cars on the road January 1st, 1862, are;*
>
> | | |
> |---|---|
> | *10 Passenger* | *5 Baggage* |
> | *61 Box* | *65 Box Merchandise Cars* |
> | *5 Lime* | *43 Platform & Coal* |
> | *12 Stone* | *13 Rack* |
> | *12 Stock* | *11 Dump or Ditching* |
> | *22 Hand* | |
>
> *The amount of wood used during the year, 6,307 cords. The number of ties used during 1861, 40,584.*

The T. Rails were iron, not steel. Pieces would break off and could not be repaired.

1862 was a good year for the Company. A long hoped for good wheat crop finally materialized and income exceeded expenses by $82,988, chiefly due to the increased freight business. President Wm. Durbin believed that many farmers had held their grain and would be shipping it the following spring, another bright prospect. Past due balances on *Domestic* bonds due in 59, 60, & 61 were paid, leaving only the *Mortgage* Bonds behind.

A new side track, 1126 feet in length, was built on *Lexington Grade*. The side track at Hunt's Mills was lengthened 482 feet, with a new switch placed at the north

Fig. 22. A double header just over the summit in 1906,

end. The side tracks at Mt. Vernon, Butler, and Shelby had their strap rail finally replaced with T. Rail. The roadbed between Ankeneytown and Butler was graveled, as was the section between Mansfield and Shelby. The Engine House at Newark was repaired, and it was reported, *that the bridge north of Fredericktown has been covered, the Howe's Truss Bridge spanning the Licking Creek, .north of St. Louisville, has been protected by placing tin roofs over the cord, both above and below.* This is the first mention of trying to weatherproof any of the bridges.

A new Wood House, 192 feet long, was built at Centerton, and while the crews were at it they repaired others at Havana, Pontiac and Prout. Extra cribbing was added at the Engine House at Huron, and still more from the Grain Warehouse to the foot bridge leading to the Light House. Lake waves were eating away at the shore line.

The docks and Grain Warehouse at Sandusky underwent change, as did the Engine House. Last, but not least, Asst. Supt. Stewart wrote, *A new self supplying Water Station has been built at Lexington Grade, and is one of the best on the road.* A little over a mile north of Lexington a water powered saw mill with a good fall of water was next to the track. Apparently they simply ran a water pipe from the mill's head race to their water tower which saved having it manned and buying pumping equipment. Filling these water towers ordinarily boiled down to two methods; hand powered or steam driven pumps. The later of course was the choice. For the year, it cost the Railroad $2,736 in wages for the water stations and $7,402 for all the engineers and firemen combined. The tower at Lexington must have looked real good to the book keepers.

Lexington grade was the section of road between the water tower and *Summit Siding*, or Alta, as it was later known. It was the steepest grade on the SM&N and north bound trains needed to have plenty of fuel, water and a good head of steam to make it. This grade was an engine killer right up to the end of the steam era.

Fig. 23. The steep grade north of Lexington led to the construction of coal docks in the late 1800s. This Photo is dated 1909.

Chapter 9

The Change of Gauge

illiam Durbin, SM&N President, died unexpectedly in May of 1863. A month earlier the Board had decided to begin planning for a change of gauge. Their road was on a five foot four inch gauge which was unlike any other railroad in Ohio, except one, the unfinished Scioto & Hocking Valley. The SM&N would adopt the standard four foot nine and one half inch spacing matching all its connecting competitors, which were listed as being four feet ten inches, called the *Ohio Gauge*. What's half an inch to a railroad? Anyway, this would allow interchanging of cars and permit through traffic to pass over the road.

Agreements with the Officers and Directors of the Baltimore & Ohio, the Central Ohio, the Cleveland & Toledo, the Michigan Southern & Northern Indiana, and the Toledo & Wabash Railroads, would form a line from Chicago to Baltimore with no interruption except crossing the Ohio River by ferry boat at Bellaire. The Sandusky Mansfield & Newark would have to change its gauge to be part of this proposed connection of roads. It was time to fish or cut bait.

The new President, C. L. Boalt, from Norwalk, and his Board of Directors had some serious planning to do. How to make the change and where to get the money were key questions they faced. Receipts had exceeded expenses by $92,000 in 1863. The Domestic Bonds were nearly paid off, but the interest on the $1,290,000 mortgage had been accumulating since January 1, 1858. It was estimated that the change of gauge, which involved narrowing the tracks and wheels on every car, would cost $80,000. Changing the engines would be another expense. In addition, four new locomotives would be needed. There would be a loss of revenue during the change, but the directors felt they could more than make up for this after the change was completed. It was decided to use $23,000 of their surplus earnings towards the gauge change, and also to close the Huron Branch, which was loosing $6,000 a year. Its rails were torn up later that summer and were to be reused on the main line.

A large portion of the expense was due to the locomotives. The fireboxes were to wide to accept the four foot nine and a half inch wheel spacing. New boilers would have to be supplied, which in some cases would cost more than the engine was worth. The Company had not taken delivery of a new locomotive since 1855, and the boilers would have to be fabricated in their own shops with the help of outside Sandusky foundries and machine shops. It was no small undertaking. Four new engines were ordered in June for $61,539 ($15,384 each) from Rogers Locomotive & Machine Works, the new name of the company after Rogers died in 1856. Morris Ketchum, one of the original partners of Rogers Ketchum & Grosvenor, had been a major stockholder in the SM&N, which may have influenced their continued use of that firm. And besides that they made damned good locomotives.

1863 had been a busy time for Superintendent Stewart. In his summery of the operating department he noted that the last of the old strap rail had been replaced and that there was 112 tons of defective T. Rail, *on hand to be re-rolled*. Evidently a mill had been set up to handle this, possibly *D. C. Henderson, Brass and Iron Pounders*, located at Jackson and Water Streets in Sandusky, or the *Liliken Steel Works*, on the south west side of town. The latter manufactured steel rails in the early 1870s, but unknown is when they started in that line.

A right of way was secured for a new faster entrance into Newark. This started about a mile and a quarter from the station and would eliminate sharp curves and steep grades that were dangerous and expensive to maintain. It would cost about $22,000. Another new track was laid at Monroeville for a connection with the Cleveland & Toledo, and separate freight and passenger stations were also erected. A new water station was built a mile north of Mansfield, and 13 miles of track between Shelby and Centerton graveled.

In the rolling stock department, Stewart noted that; *In preparing for business on the new gauge, four of your locomotives are already in process of being changed. The Mt. Vernon, a passenger engine has been completed. The Knox, suitable for very light work, is nearly so. The boiler of the Mohican and Independence are nearly finished. The trucks of 17 box cars and 3 platform cars have been changed to the narrow gauge and loaned to the Central Ohio Road for transporting Baltimore and Chicago freights between Newark and Bellair. One passenger car, 17 box cars, 8 platform and coal cars, 8 ditching cars and 9 hand cars have been built during the year.*

Stewart estimated that he would need 75 new box cars and 25 new platform cars to meet the needs of the coming business. 47 old box cars and 5 platform cars needed rebuilding. The freight and passenger cars were of mostly wood construction, including some of the trucks. Vibration and weather took a toll on the life span of these cars, and caused continuing maintenance expense.

The change of gauge was to take place in the spring of 1864, *as soon as the frost was out of the ground.* So much to do, so little time!

The change began on March the 5th with the assistance of track crews borrowed from neighboring railroads. The Central Ohio, the Cleveland Columbus and Cincinnati, the Michigan Southern & Northern Indiana, and the Toledo & Wabash Railroads each sent crews. The March 4th edition of the *Sandusky Register* best described preparations:

Unless some unexpected drawback should occur, work will begin tomorrow (Saturday) evening, after the passage of trains for the day. A large force of workman has been engaged, and the change will be made as rapidly as possible. The men will begin at Newark, working northward. There will be no interruption of passenger trains of the road, except that the Mansfield train may be discontinued for a few days that will be needed to make the change from Mansfield here. There will be as little interruption of the local freight business as possible; and it is expected that the entire work will be completed inside of twenty days.

One of the new locomotives received from Patterson, ("Newark" by name,) with the "Mt. Vernon," one of the old ones altered to suit the new gauge, left here on Wednesday, going via Berea, Columbus and the Central Ohio Road. The "Knox," a small engine for switching, also rebuilt and narrowed, will go down on a platform car. Passenger cars (narrow) have been provided at the south end to run daily to whatever point the work may have reached, where they will be met by trains of the old gauge and transfers made. When the work is finished, all the wide gauge rolling stock and machinery will be left at this end of the route where it will be rebuilt and put into use again.

The prospects for a large increase of freight business over this line, when changed and in order again, are very flattering. During the winter, the amount of through freight from Chicago eastward transferred at Monroeville and Newark, has been much larger than was looked for and there is now a heavy accumulation at Newark, owing to the fact that it was necessary to get all there was on the way there, before breaking gauge.

The careful planning paid off. Everything went smooth and faster than hoped for. The March 16, 1864 edition of the *Sandusky Register* carried another story:

Superintendent Stewart announced yesterday that the change of gauge was completed this morning on the SM&N Railroad, and that trains would leave the city on the new gauge for Newark this morning (15th). The change of gauge commenced some ten days since, has been pressed forward with great energy, despite unfavorable weather, and has been affected in an extraordinarily short space of time. To Mr. Stewart, much credit is due for pressing forward of the work, and for its speedy and successful completion. The first regular trains running through on the new gauge today, will mark a new era in the importance and prosperity of this road, or we will be very much mistaken.

On Saturday March 19, 1864 fifteen cars of the Michigan Southern & Northern Indiana Railroad, from Chicago destined for Baltimore, entered the SM&N tracks at Monroeville and made their way down the line to Newark and the Central Ohio.

At the beginning of 1864 the SM&N owned eleven locomotives. One of these was the *Licking*, which was not worth changing. The *Knox*, which was very small, had been changed along with the *Mt. Vernon*, a passenger engine. The latter was originally built narrow and then widened, and was changed back rather easily. The Knox and Mt. Vernon, along with two new engines ones which arrived in January, the *Newark*, (2nd) and the *Mansfield* (2nd), were the only engines on the road when the change was completed. The last of the four new engines ordered, the *Frederick* (2nd) and the *Monroeville*, did not arrive at Sandusky until the 23rd of March.

To make maters interesting, the *Knox* and the *Mt. Vernon* were involved in a head on wreck. One was pulling a gravel train and the other a passenger. It was the end of the line for the *Knox*, whose conductor had looked at his watch wrong. The *Mt. Vernon* needed major repair and the shops were full. By the end of the year three more old locomotives would join the fleet, the 35 ton 4-6-0 *Mohican* (one of the two largest engines owned), the *Shelby*, and the *Independence*. That left the SM&N with only seven engines to do the work of the road and forced the Directors to rent a locomotive from the Cleveland & Toledo Railroad.

In January 1865 Superintendent Stewart would report:

Two other of the old locomotives are in the process of re-construction, the "Plymouth", and "Lexington." The boiler of the "Plymouth" is half finished, and the tender ready for the frame and trucks. The boiler of the "Lexington" is ready for frame.

Of 139 box and stock cars, 31 of them are new, 21 having been built in our shops at Sandusky, and 10 in Detroit. The trucks and axles of the rest of the rolling stock have been change from the old to the new gauge, the bodies thoroughly repaired, making the cars almost as good as new.

Two new caboose cars were added to the fleet, the first ever mentioned. The rail cars were of wood construction, cheap, light weight, and easy to build.

A new water tower was built at Shelby Junction, with water supplied by the Cleveland Columbus and Cincinnati Railroads stationary steam engine at their tower. The usual bridge and track construction was carried on even though the change had exceeded estimates. Major expenses were;

Change of gauge	$88,823
Four new locomotives	$61,539
Rebuild 3 old locomotives	$27,800
Narrow rolling stock	$9,650
Hire C&T Locomotives	$2,116
New shop tools required	$1,000
2800 Bu. Wheat	$3,542

In October, one of their passenger trains derailed on a curve three miles north of Shelby. A well known German Physician going from Shelby to Plymouth to see a patient was killed. Doctor C. W. Crall had been standing on the platform of the baggage car and fell between it and the next car. As the editor of the *Mansfield Herald* delicately put it, *He was instantly crushed, some of the iron went through his bowels, broke his left shoulder and arm all to fragments, and tore out part of his liver.* The Railroad settled with his widow for $1,500. The news story surely must have helped her lawyer win her case. When employees lost their life there was no compensation.

Fig. 24. One of the last SM&N engines turned over to the B&O. The fancy paint trim suggests it may have been the "Sandusky". The 1870s photograph was taken on the turn table at Sandusky. Note the ship mast to the right. Courtesy of the Coleman Collection, Ohio Historical Society.

Chapter 10

The Struggle to Survive

The financial picture looked better after the change, but there were still problems for the Directors to face. The bottom line would hold them hostage.

	1864	1865
Gross Earnings	$382,807	$421,916
Net earnings	$189,407	$166,133

The profits were down in 1865 for two reasons. First, there was a severe shortage of cars as some of their rolling stock passed off loaded to connecting roads, something they had not experienced before. The SM&N had more local freight business than cars available to handle the demand. Secondly, the Civil War had disrupted, and partially destroyed, parts of the Baltimore & Ohio Railroad for weeks at a time; this had a chain reaction effect on the SM&N.

Part of the expenses for 1865 were listed in the SM&N Annual report:

One baggage car	$2,000
Four box cars @$900	$3,600
Fifteen coal cars @800	$12,000
Two Engines, changed	$22,000
New station at Prout	$600
Re-shingle Grain Warehouse	$1,837
Grain shortage at Warehouse	$5,057

The road had used 9,841 cords of wood during the year.

There were now nine locomotives on the road, including the two that had been narrowed and rebuilt, the *Lexington* and *Plymouth*. It was stated in the annual report that *the boiler of the "Sandusky* is nearly complete and some of the machinery prepared for the same. This engine we hope to have out by the first of next August." That projection turned out to be wishful thinking.

The *Sandusky* wouldn't hit the rails until February of 1868! It cost approximately $11,000 each to rebuild these engines, which tied up shops and manpower. The new ones were being delivered for a little over $15,000. This must have caused a little head scratching. It had been determined that the *Mt. Vernon* was not worth repairing and the *Erie*, built in 1855, and *Hocking*, built in 1853, were put into storage.

Operations in the year 1866 were somewhat better except for three bridges that washed out near St. Louisville by floods in September. One washed out, was rebuilt temporarily, and washed out again a week later. New masonry abutments had to be placed on pilings due to quicksand in the area, and these bridges had been described as the weak spot in the whole line. Temporary bridges on pilings would get the line open until Howe Trusses of 125 and 110 feet respectively, could be shipped from Worcester, Massachusetts and set in place. It was also recommended that some of the existing bridges, *be covered with iron or tin.*

With seeming pride Superintendent Stewart reported that 7,160 rails had been mended in the Company's Shops at an expense of 75 cents per rail. This was the first mention of doing their own.

Work continued on the *Sandusky*. Meanwhile the Company bought two new passenger coaches with raised roofs, and they built a similar car in their own shops along with a baggage car, 3 stock, 3 box, and 10 coal cars. Their car shop must have employed a good sized crew. Unfortunately three of its platform cars, loaded with oil, caught fire between Mansfield and Newark and were a total loss.

A new scale was built in Newark and a similar one was needed at Mansfield, where business with connecting railroads had increased by one third since 1865. Mansfield was becoming a manufacturing center, and its freight and passenger income looked promising.

In one reported accident a man hunting in the marshes north of Mansfield had one leg cut off when struck by a locomotive. No explanation was given as to how it happened. Perhaps he had a gun and a jug, one was loaded, the other empty.

At the end of 1867 President Boalt gave a somewhat grim financial report, but still made an effort to bolster the spirits of the stock and bond holders. He noted that the interest had not been paid on the mortgage of $1,290,000 for six and one half years. The accumulated debt now stood at $2,020,752.75! He apparently finally gave up on the wheat crops and turned his eyes south to the coal fields and the unfinished Scioto & Hocking Valley Railroad. It had been graded years before and went broke before much of anything else was done. In glowing terms Boalt expressed the dream that if it was completed 25 miles from Newark to Somerset, *the workable coal fields lie south of Somerset from ten to eighteen miles, and are remarkable for their purity, thickness and the ease that they may be worked.* The coal burned brightly, and left little ash, it was claimed.

He also advanced the belief that iron ore abounded in those hills. Coupled with the coal, he felt a bright manufacturing future would spring up in towns along the line. A committee of Board members was appointed to meet with the stockholders to see if money could be subscribed for a rail extension. In September of 1867 the committee met at the Court House in Newark with a delegation from the proposed Newark Somerset & Straitsville Railroad. The idea must not have burned brightly as the coal in the minds of the shareholders. The answer was no. The SM&N was in to deep already.

J. H. Stewart resigned in June of 1866, and H. F. Paden was appointed Master of Transportation. In his first end of the year report, issued in January of 1867, he noted that a gravel pit had been opened at Vanatta's Station and 10 miles of track from Utica southward were thoroughly ballasted. A gravel train stationed at that end of the line from June to September also graveled two miles of track between Bellville and Butler from a pit near Lexington. Other sections were done as needed. Getting the cross ties out of the mud would increase their life span.

112 tons of new rail, along with 1200 tons of repaired T. Rail were laid. The repaired rails consisted of, *old iron mended and spliced in the company's shops at Sandusky, at an expense of eighty cents per rail....Should more fires be added there and a larger amount of old iron mended, less new would need to be purchased.*

The permanent bridges at St. Louisville were finished in the summer of 1867, and parts of the bridges swept away in the flood were recovered and put up at Bellville. Two other bridges at Monroeville and Pontiac were repaired and *the tin roofs repaired in an improved shape, painted, and otherwise placed in complete order.*

Two of the locomotives broke a driving axle with one of them suffering some serious damage. Both were repaired and put back in service. The SM&N had nine engines on the road and were still tinkering with the *Sandusky*.

TABLE E.

Satement showing Mileage, and Use of Oil and Tallow by Locomotives and Engineers for year 1864.

1864 NAMES.	Miles	Galls. Oil.	Lbs. Tallow.	Miles to 1 Pt. Oil.	Miles to 1 lb Tallow.	1864 NAMES.	Miles	Galls. Oil.	Lbs. Tallow.	Miles to 1 Pt. Oil.	Miles to 1 lb Tallow.
Plymouth..........old	8178	17½	140	58-4	58-4	Stephen Clark	36245	124¾	844	36-3	50
Independence.....new	21972	74¾	354	36-7	62-1	H. H. Elwell...........	19214	55¼	401	44-2	48
Sandusky..........old	4843	17½	126	34-6	38-4	James Clark	31008	122¾	856	31-5	36-2
Shelby............new	5816	19¾	156	36-8	38	James Almond........	29762	141	849	26-3	35-4
Erie ....old	5010	22	104	28-5	48-1	Samuel F. Jones.......	9355	44½	158	26	59-2
Lexington ....old	4509	20¼	64	27-1	70	Robert Hogg	18447	82	480	28-1	38-4
Hocking ....old	6178	21	174	36-8	35-5	R. Salsbury...........	19354	91¾	583	26-3	33-2
Knox ....new	8657	54	190	20	45-5	J. Dill	7556	42¾	188	22	40-2
Frederick.........new	30127	136¾	883	27-7	34	J. A. Koeglie.........	1634	7	36	29	45-4
Mt. Vernon........new	20100	66½	487	37-7	41-2	C. & T. Engineers.....	12580	42	344	37-4	36-5
Mansfield.........new	25874	110¾	793	29	32-6	John H. Smith.	19608	91	672	26-9	29-1
Newark...........new	26278	125¾	851	26	30-9	Henry Fisher..........	198	¾	6	32	32
Monroeville.......new	24541	111½	844	27-5	28	Chas. Hardwidge......	300	9	50		
Gratton ....C. & T.	12854	42	304	38-2	42-2	George Pollock	3752	17½	112	26	33-5
Mohican ....new	4134	32	100	16-1	41-3						
	209011	872	5570	30	37-5		209011	872	5570	30	37-5

Fig. 25. Table E. Mileage an d use of Oil and Tallow.

Table F.

Showing number of way passengers carried from Stations on S. M. & N. R. R., for year 1865.

	SANDUSKY.	PERUE.	MONROEVILLE.	PONTIAC.	HAVANA.	CENTERTON.	NEW HAVEN.	PLYMOUTH.	SHELBY.	MANSFIELD.	LEXINGTON.	BELLEVILLE.	INDEPENDENCE.	ANKNEYTOWN.	FREDERICK.	MT. VERNON.	UTICA.	LOUISVILLE.	NEWARK.	TOTAL.
January ..	1,627	185	2,249	85	283	295	68	525	1,382	2,369	343	426	167	73	560	1,320	297	122	1,303	13,642
February..	2,137	204	2,169	61	284	366	70	655	1,404	2,581	375	537	240	112	586	1,437	456	122	1,466	15,264
March	1,862	226	2,703	134	337	397	92	672	1,895	3,108	542	583	373	106	800	1,906	626	155	1,770	18,294
April.....:	1,288	179	2,115	60	263	349	54	565	1,439	3,611	365	453	228	101	638	1,581	403	128	1,286	15,103
May	1,280	169	2,184	63	301	335	55	509	1,651	2,431	356	445	205	71	530	1,528	440	106	1,251	13,915
June	1,451	139	2,063	41	216	314	85	698	1,802	2,662	435	531	187	74	503	1,465	340	82	1,466	14,558
July	1,737	167	2,165	74	271	381	62	759	1,908	3,246	571	663	383	150	580	1,948	443	127	1,578	17,217
August....	1,626	187	2,847	65	273	347	76	881	2,317	3,654	599	783	299	157	851	2,055	483	154	1,781	19,440
September	1,432	194	2,774	62	294	427	61	1,672	2,224	3,347	513	532	329	108	1,056	2,012	470	166	1,786	18,861
October ..	1,651	218	2,929	56	335	355	84	908	1,860	3,860	546	727	329	89	607	1,745	541	132	1,638	18,613
November.	1,179	120	2,512	72	263	300	112	671	1,725	2,808	495	566	312	166	780	1,484	354	68	1,515	15,507
December.	1,065	212	2,220	82	309	341	62	621	1,421	3,033	587	702	312	97	697	1,633	439	93	1,311	15,140

Fig. 26. Table F Mileage and Use of Oil and Tallow.

Chapter 11

The Last Year

Unknown to the general public, 1868 was to be the last full year of operation by the Sandusky Mansfield & Newark Railroad. In his financial report President Boalt calculated the road's debt at $2,307,314.50. The earnings had increased but never at a level that would cover operating expenses, mortgage payments, rail line maintenance, and constant bridge replacement. There was a shortage of engines, and in spite of the efforts of their own car building shops, there were never enough cars to handle the demand. Delays on their tracks backed up connecting through traffic. The SM&N was the weak link in the Chicago to Baltimore chain.

However, one bright spot in 1868 was the completion in February of the engine *Sandusky*; it had taken nearly four years. Under a headline "A Splendid Locomotive", the February 17, edition of the *Sandusky Register* carried this account:

> *The Engine "Sandusky," of the Sandusky, Mansfield & Newark Railroad, makes its first trip before the express train that leaves at 9:05 this morning. This engine has lately been rebuilt in the shops of the Company and is conceded to be the finest locomotive that has been turned out in our city. In rebuilding it was found necessary to virtually make a new engine, and every important part of her is entirely new. She weighs about 26 tons, and when put on trial Saturday last, behaved splendidly, making the distance from Monroeville to Sandusky in twenty eight minutes. The veteran engineer, Clark, will preside at her foot board, and will doubtless win new honors for himself. As a work of art we would cordially commend this new engine to the art loving citizens of our city; the painting alone being worth a trip to the Mansfield Depot. Her machine work was done under the superintendent Mr. John Y. Beatte, foreman of the shop, and painting by William A. Purden.*

Mr. H. F. Paden, still *Master of Transportation*, gave a lengthy report on the work on the road and rolling stock during 1868. He felt that the year had been attended with a good degree of success, safety, and efficiency.

In addition to the *Sandusky*, which was back on the road, he listed repairs to the other rolling stock.

The large ten-wheeled engine "Mohican" has had a new set of iron tires put on, and received a thorough overhauling. One of your passenger engines (Independence) met with a serious accident in February, by breaking both driving axles. She was torn to pieces badly, but has been refitted and put in good order in all respects. Two other engines (Plymouth and Lexington) have receive general repairs - a new driving axle being put under the former, and the latter supplied with a new flue-sheet and tubes.

On the four freight engines purchased at the time of gauge change, as much extra work has been done as could be consistent with the demands made upon them for service during the busy season. These engines have been worked to their utmost capacity, and need more or less extensive repairs.

One of the pressing needs of the Company is a small or "pony" engine for switching at Sandusky. This work, which is yearly growing in magnitude, could be done with much greater economy by an engine especially adapted for it than by the larger machines we are now compelled to use.

In the car department, one new baggage car, one mail and passenger car, (rebuilt) and five new platform cars have been turned out. Five more platforms are being built. There have been condemned and broken up, six box freight cars and six platforms. The present equipment is summed up as follows;

For passenger trains;
4   Baggage and Express cars
3   Mail and Passenger cars
9   Passenger Coaches (two very old)

For Freight Trains;
3   *Caboose cars*
78 *Box Grain and Merchandise cars*
6   *Old Box or Lime cars*
20 *Stock cars*
50 *Coal cars*
15 *Platform cars (Good)*
11 *Platform cars (Old)*

An increase in the number of passenger cars is much needed, and arrangements have been made for building two in our shops, though work has not begun on either.

A much needed improvement has been made at Sandusky, in the enlarging and thorough repairing of the old engine house, A new dockage was built back and under it, the entire building raised and placed on substantial stone foundations, with room for another track added. In short, a building which a year ago threatened to tumble down at any moment, has been converted into a more convenient, safe and comfortable shelter for our locomotives than any other owned by the Company. It has stalls for five engines, pits walled and floored with stone and amply drained, is well warmed and lighted, and in every respect fitted up to last for years.

New water houses have been built at Pontiac and Mt. Vernon, with windmills for pumping; a windmill has also been put on the water house at Plymouth. New passenger platforms have been put down at Centerton and Frederick, and a new stock yard, for loading live stock, built at Independence. An additional siding has been laid at Mansfield, the business of which point is constantly increasing.

At Mt. Vernon, the station building has been enlarged by 20 feet, to afford an office for the United States Express Company, that Company paying the expense of the enlargement. This building as it now stands, is of greater value than any other similar building owned by the Company, outside of Sandusky. One of the main sidings at Newark has been lengthened out from the depot westward, giving additional room that was much needed. A track has also been laid from the main line, north of the canal bridge, along the canal as far as Second Street in Newark, for the purpose of chiefly receiving coal from boats. Though not much business has been derived from this track as was anticipated, the indirect benefits from it have been considerable, in stimulating increased shipments of coal over your line from mines located on other lines of other railroads running into Newark.

He reported that there was a shortage of side track space at Mt. Vernon, and coal shipments were increasing. Cars destined for there were sometimes placed at other stations for days waiting for available side track space. Many of the telegraph poles were rotting off at ground level and were simply sawed off and reset. Fuel consumption was 9,141 cords of wood, up from 7,682 the year before. This was attributed to the running of one more engine (Sandusky), and the use of the engine for switching at Sandusky. Although hauling coal they were still burning wood.

A 600-foot long trestle, five miles north of Newark, with an average height of 27 feet was filled. This had been referred to as another weak spot in the line and had caused numerous interruptions over the years. 42,561 cross ties had been replaced (about the usual average per year), and 134 ½ tons of new rail laid. Paden's crews laid 1 ½ miles of new rails of "the fish joint pattern" north of Independence and south of Springmill. In addition, "twelve and one forth miles of spliced iron, or old rails with the worn spots cut out and pieces again spliced into long rails at the Company's shops, have been put into the track at various places. The welded joints rarely break and the track is greatly benefited...by the removal of slivered and pounded pieces." Besides this work, four miles of track between Bellville and Independence, and three miles of the steep grade leading south out of Mansfield, were ballasted and new ties installed.

The Mansfield grade was a tough one for south bound engineers. From a standing start little speed could be gained before entering the grade. It embarrassed numerous train crews for nearly a century. Summit Siding (Alta), with an elevation of 1287 feet, was the highest point between Newark (867 feet) and Lake Erie (601 feet). Mansfield, at 1150 feet, and Lexington, at 1180 feet, were at the base of the what were rather steep inclines of only a little over a mile in length. A helper engine was stationed at Lexington to push trains north up to Alta until shortly before World War I, when the heavier and more powerful Baldwin Class Q-1c and USRA Q3 2-8-2 Light Mikado engines came on line to replace older freight locomotives. Similar support may have been required at Mansfield.

Adam Hively had a blacksmith shop a short distance south of Alta. When the railroad refused to pay for a cow it killed Hively coated the rails with soap and grease. The next north bound freight stalled amid slipping wheels, thundering exhausts, and a cursing engine crew. Unable to restart the train had to be broken into sections, taken to Alta or Mansfield, and reassembled, causing a serious delay. The railroad figured out what happened and had Hively arrested.

The bridges on both sides of St. Louisville were roofed with tin in 1868, as were two more between Bellville and Independence. A new trestle bridge, 198 feet long, was built at Vannatta's Station (Company's Spelling).

There were casualties on the rails that year. A six-year-old girl named Catherine Guiker was killed at Independence in June by being run over by a freight train backing up. Unseen by anyone she was swinging on the rear platform of a passenger car attached to a freight train when she lost her hold and fell under the wheels. O. A. Rice, a brake man, was killed while riding on top of one of the cars on September 1st. He was struck by Belt's bridge south of Utica and died the next day. Two weeks later in Sandusky a seven-and-a-half-year-old boy was riding on the platform of a mail car being switched when it collided with a car load of lumber being pushed by employees of Ryan Johnson & Co. The boy fell off the platform and was killed when he fell under the wheels. A railroad yard was a dangerous playground.

Fig. 27. Fireman Albert Gore (left) and engineer Jack Cline with helper engine 965 at Lexington sometime around 1909. Cline was later killed by lightening, but details are lacking. Both men lived within sight of the station, and could walk to work.

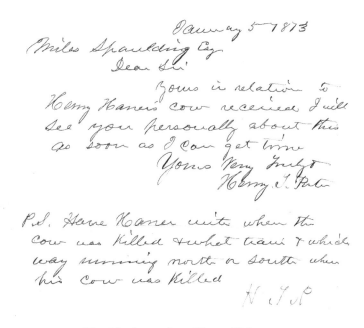

Fig. 28. Letter from Henry Hainer.

Fig. 29. The letter was addressed to Miles Spaulding.

Fig. 30. In September of 1886, a run away horse was killed when it was struck by a Winans Camel in a bridge near Butler. The engine derailed and struck the bridge which broke under the impact. Engineer William Staggers was pinned against the hot boiler by a beam and roasted there for nearly four hours until freed by a section gang. He died half an hour after being carried to the Butler Station.

Chapter 12

The Lease of the SM&N

The Directors and Stockholders of the SM&N met on January 20, 1869 to review the operations of the previous year. The shortage of rolling stock, the mounting debt, and the heavy operating expenses must have worn their patience. The following month, on February 13, 1869, the Sandusky Mansfield & Newark Railroad was leased to the Central Ohio Railroad. Out of a total of 18,000 shares, 13,938 shares were represented at the stockholders meeting, and the vote was unanimous for the lease. The lease was to begin on July 1, 1869, was to run for a period of seventeen years and five months, and could be renewed for two additional 20 year terms.

The B&O was required to keep the line, rolling stock, buildings, bridges and locomotives in as good order as they had received them, or replace with items of equal value at the end of the lease. The SM&N was to pay for building additions and improvements which increased the value of their property. The B&O received 13 locomotives (3 of which were stored wide gauge), 9 passenger cars, 7 baggage, and 185 freight cars of all types.

Five years later, the B&O had 31 locomotives, 20 passenger cars, 34 mail, baggage, and caboose cars, and 600 freight cars on the road. The SM&N could never have matched that.

In January of 1872 the B&O leased and completed the Newark Somerset & Straitsville Railroad which was being finished into the coal fields to the south of Newark. This project had taken nearly 20 years and left a trail of devastated investors, most of which were from Newark and Licking County. It was estimated the original graded but unfinished line from Newark to Somerset could be purchased for as little as $15,000 from the original investors. Preparing the line for rails from Newark to Straitsville was projected to cost $250,000. Owners of large coal acreage offered cash and half interest in 2,800 acres of rich coal fields if the line was completed.

The B&O now had a cheap source of coal which would fuel its line for years to come, and greatly increase its freight income.

Fig. 31. A north bound engine at Fredericktown in 1872. Note the bridge, mill dam and warehouse buildings. The white building behind the engine may have been an early station. Photo from the Carl Winegardner Collection.

Chapter 13

The Port of Sandusky

Sandusky was blessed with a natural harbor. It was rather shallow with a shifting sand bar at its entrance, but offered protection from the wild storm waves of Lake Erie. Originally identified as *Ogontz Place*, after an Indian who roamed there, a small plat was laid out on the south shore in 1816 and named Portland. Two years later it was enlarged and re-named Sandusky City. Years later the town was still often referred to as Portland. The small population of 300 in 1820 doubled by 1830, and grew to 1,500 by 1840, 5,000 in 1850, and 10,000 by 1855. It was a boom town.

The harbor was a stopping point for lake sailing ships, and quite naturally it became center of early commerce. Wagon traffic made its way from towns 100 miles or more to the south and south west. Wet lands west of Sandusky and the Great Black Swamp made land travel towards Toledo extremely difficult in rainy seasons. This made the option of lake passage much more desirable.

Lake schooners and smaller sloops were making regular stops at Sandusky and other ports along the lake. The first steamboat, *Walk in The Water*, was a slow, primitive craft that was storm wrecked near Buffalo in 1820 after six years of operation. Built in Buffalo it had ushered in a new era of boat building design. Schooners with a normal displacement of 28 to 35 tons in 1822 were dwarfed by the arrival of the new steamboat *Superior* with a displacement of 346 tons. The boiler of the "Superior" had been salvaged from the *Walk in the Water*, drug from the beach wreckage overland on rollers across a peninsula after trees were felled, and installed in the new boat. Superior was a side wheeler, and all passenger cabins were below deck. The first steamer with an upper deck was the *Great Western*, built in 1838. It had masts with sails that assisted during favorable winds.

In 1823 a total of 178 ships docked at Sandusky. The *Superior* alone stopped 43 times. Two years later 286 made port, and the number increased yearly. The steamboat *General Vance* made three trips a week from Sandusky to Lower Sandusky (Fremont) on the Sandusky River with stops between.

In the summer of 1849 the citizens voted for a tax to purchase a dredging machine for use in the shallow bars in the harbor. The $6,000 machine came from Buffalo and was horse powered, that is horses walking a tread mill to provide power for the machinery. The *Daily Sanduskian* commented that two small engines with locomotive boilers could be installed for $3,000 and save having to use a steam boat to accompany the dredge. Two scoops swiveled to dump sand and mud into scows along side which were equipped with trap doors in the bottoms for unloading. The shifting sand bars became a problem as ships grew larger.

The February 23, 1847 issue of the *Buffalo Commercial Advertiser* contained a list of 55 brigs, schooners, propellers, and steamboats being built on Lake Erie, amounting to 13,200 tons. Sandusky's boat yards were part of this total.

The opening of Sandusky's two railroads brought even more ships to accommodate the freight and passenger business, with several being owned or controlled by rail lines. If you wanted to go to New York or the east coast the boats were the way to go. It wasn't unusual to see six to ten boats a day enter or depart the docks. Lake travel was not without its hazards however. The lake bottoms must be littered with wreckage.

In 1823 the schooner *Sylph* left Sandusky for Detroit and sank off North Bass Island with all aboard. Three years later the schooner "Morning Star" went down off Middle Bass Island with loss of two crewmen. The Steamer *Chesapeake* and the schooner *J. Porter* collided in July of 1847. Everyone on the *Porter* climbed aboard the larger steamer figuring the schooner would sink. Both took on water and the *Chesapeake* started for shore but her fires were soon flooded and both went down in forty feet of water. The upper cabin parted from the hull and to this, plus doors and planks, survivors hung in the rough waters. Seventy some passengers and crew were saved by the steamer "Harrison", which came to their rescue.

As traffic grew so did the accident rate. The January 12, 1850 edition of the *Daily Sanduskian* carried a list of ship wrecks on all the Great Lakes during 1849. There were 97 vessels either involved in collisions, ran aground, capsized in storms, lost rigging, dumped cargo, or were sunk during the year. 34 lives were lost and damage to cargo and ships amounted to $368,171. The previous year 55 lives were lost, and damages amounted to $420,512.

A major loss occurred in June of 1850 when the steamer *Griffith* caught fire 20 miles west of Cleveland on its way to Sandusky. It went down with nearly 300 lives lost. Of 154 bodies recovered the next day 94 were buried in a common grave 40 feet long by 6 feet wide. Some of these were immigrants with no identification or family. That same June the boiler on the *General Wayne* blew up near Vermillion with a loss of about 50. These hazards must have weighed heavily on the minds of railroad passengers arriving in Sandusky for transfer to ships. Rail travel must have looked safer.

Chapter 14

The SM&N Freight
& Passender Business

The freight handled in the late 1840s is somewhat surprising. Salt, a necessary staple in frontier Ohio, was imported in large quantities (11,000 barrels in 1849), along with manufactured merchandise from the east and Europe. As early 1843 the Milan firm of Smith Hyde & Walker advertised for 100,000 bushels of wheat for spring shipment, which they would exchange for 3,000 barrels of fine and 1,000 barrels of coarse salt, and 500 barrels of fish. Boats unloaded pig iron, lumber, iron ore, and even barrels of oysters found their way into Sandusky's docks.

The biggest exports delivered by the Sandusky Mansfield & Newark were wheat, corn, flour, pork, beef, and whisky. The latter item may seem strange, but corn could be ground at the local gristmill, run through a distillery, and shipped in barrels. Whisky was readily salable and easier to transport than bulk corn. In 1834 Richland County alone had 34 distilleries, "in blast", as the temperance people used to say. The SM&N hauled a lot of whisky north to Sandusky (6,236 barrels in 1850). When the line opened further south in 1851 the amount must have doubled. Henry Smith had a large commercial distillery in Newark and put many of the small local operators out of business. As late as 1861, Smith was shipping nearly 4000 barrels a year north on the SM&N. This was in addition to an unknown amount by the Ohio & Erie Canal and the Central Ohio Railroad. It had to be one of the biggest operations in the state, but the Licking County histories, written during the temperance movement, make no mention of him or his business. Not all of the booze that arrived in Sandusky made it on board the boats. In 1869 Sandusky could boast of 84 saloons, 20 were located in one square block downtown. Quite naturally the local law enforcement officers were able to keep the jail well occupied.

While the whisky was going north beer was headed south. Sandusky had a very large German population, estimated at 25% in 1867. The German language was taught in public schools and used in church services until World War One when it fell out of favor. Quite naturally they liked beer, the favorite drink of the old country. In the early 1850s Philip Dauch and Vincenz Fox each built breweries, with the latter being operated by Anton Ilg for many years. The Phenix Brewery opened in 1850 and advertised the best beer, ale, and porter this side of Philadelphia. Much of this beer went south on the SM&N and the Mad River. Monroeville had three distilleries and a brewery from which they could ship on two railroads, the SM&N or the Cleveland & Toledo going north, south, east or west. No production records exist, but 3,365 barrels of something left town on the SM&N in 1866.

A Mr. F .Reisheimer advertised 3,000 gallons of Catawba Wine, vintage 1863, in February of 1864. There were 24 small wineries as early as 1855 in the Sandusky area and on the islands. The wine industry was beginning.

In the 1850s a 40 ½ gallon barrel of whisky sold for $12.00, and beer was $5.00 to $8.00 per barrel depending on type. The wooden barrels were worth fifty cents each and the SM&N hauled 203 car loads of barrel staves to cooper shops along the line in 1865.

Most small towns on the line had a foundry. Vannatta, Fredericktown, Bellville and Plymouth each had impressive operations for their size. Coal, coke and pig iron were in demand for these. Newark, Mt. Vernon and Mansfield each developed heavy industries and were dependent on the railroad. Mt. Vernon received 601 tons of pig iron in 1866, the most of any, much of which went to the Cooper & Clark Foundry. The demand for coal kept the SM&N cars busy along the line in the late 1860s. Although the SM&N delivered coal in increasing amounts each year, (8,144 tons in 1866), its engines continued to burn wood. The coal was more expensive and not yet available in large quantities.

Apples and cider were among seasonal farm produce shipped. An old account book from the Englehart General Store in Lexington indicates that the firm shipped 683 barrels of cider to Chicago in a three month period in 1855. Two cooperage's in Bellville furnished 503 barrels at fifty cents each, which must have arrived by rail. Some of the many orchards all along the Clear Fork valley could trace their origin to seedlings from Johnny Appleseed. Englehart sold the cider for $2.00 per barrel plus the cost of the barrel for which he received a twenty five cent commission.

Local specialties from each stop on the SM&N created a varied freight. Wool from Utica and Fredericktown, butter and rye from Plymouth, lumber from Centerton, potatoes from Bellville, and fish from Huron, were just a few of these.

The Sandusky waterfront had numerous docks a pier. The Mad River & Lake Erie and the Cleveland & Toledo Railroads each had facilities along with passenger stations. Warehouses, mercantile shops, taverns and hotels lined the waterfront, and business boomed with the ships and trains that gave Sandusky life in the 1850s and 1860s. However, the railroads that had given the waterfront and the city it's vitality, would also take part of it away as they became more connected with the east coast lines in the 1880s. The railroads ran year around, the lake was frozen in winter.

Summer tourist traffic boosted passenger income for the SM&N and the Mad River and Lake Erie as resorts were established on the islands and large pleasure steamers became popular in the 1870s, 80s, and beyond. Sandusky gained a reputation as a beautiful resort area; this reputation would grow through the years. Special "Excursion" trains became popular and boosted revenue during the summer vacation season.

Fig. 32. Pictured is the B&O Grain Warehouse on the center pier at Sandusky. The long dock could accommodate several ships at once. The building burned in 1883. Photo courtesy the Sandusky Public Library.

Chapter 15

The Baltimore and Ohio Takes Over

The B&O took control of the SM&N on July 1, 1869. Named the Lake Erie Division of the B&O, H. Paden, former Master of Transportation of the SM&N, was named Manager of both leased lines, that is the SM&N and the Central Ohio. C. W. Quincy, former Master of Transportation on the Central Ohio, was named General Manager. It was announced the car shops would remain in Sandusky

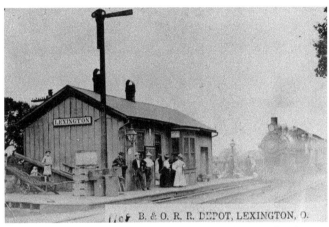

Fig 33. The 1871 passenger and telegraph depot at Lexington was one of the first built when the B&O leased the SM&N. It was typical of small town stations of that period.

with an increased work force as the B&O found they could build the wooden cars cheaper there than at Zanesville or Baltimore. All employees and officers would remain except for the Board of Directors.

The B&O fiscal year always ended on September 30th. On that date in 1871 the Lake Erie Division had net income of $513,786, and a net profit of $97,857. An enormous amount of rebuilding had been carried out and no doubt affected the bottom line. Long lists of improvements were included in the stockholders report. A few of notable the improvements were;

At Newark water station 2,575 feet of six inch water line was laid from the canal to the water station insuring a natural flow of water. Six stone culverts were built including a large one at Fredericktown. At Dry Creek, one of the perennial weak spots, new stone abutments and a *Bollman* iron superstructure replaced the old bridge. This was the first iron bridge on the line. New *frost proof* water stations were built at Monroeville, Shelby Junction, and Butler, with the Monroeville station getting a brick fire proof power house (12 X 36) with a 635 foot water line to the Huron River. Butler was fed with 1,200 feet of 3 inch line from the Clear Fork.

79

At Plymouth a new 30 X 80 grain warehouse was built, able to handle 3,000 bushels a day. A new 18 X 33 passenger and telegraph depot was built at Lexington, and the, *unsafe and unsightly projection over the warehouse tracks removed.* At Fredericktown a large warehouse was purchased and moved to a point nearer the tracks, and part of the building converted into a passenger waiting room. At Mt. Vernon the interior of the waiting room was *remodeled and fitted up in modern style.* At Newark four stalls for engines, 20 X 60 each, were built, and a 6 X 9 water tub fed with 611 feet of pipe was installed. It's interesting to note that some Newark improvements were listed with Central Ohio Division and others listed under Lake Erie, both in the same building.

Newark was destined to play a much more important roll with the B&O due to its central location.

Fig. 34. Early water stations had steam driven pumps. Gas engines later replaced them. Note the fancy brick work on the frost proof pump house.

At Sandusky a new 407 X 60 solid dock with tracks laid was built so that lumber and ore could be unloaded from vessels more easily. Construction on a 25 X 600 dock for loading coal to ships was started.

Not directly connected with the Lake Erie Division, but of great importance, was the completion of two bridges over the Ohio River. One opened between Parkersburg and the Marietta road, and the other between Bellaire, on the Central Ohio Division, and Wheeling, on the Main Line, at a cost of $2,337,156. These would insure unbroken travel from east to west and eliminate ferries over the Ohio River. President John Garrett was bent on expanding and improving the B&O and beating the competition.

In September of 1872 a head on wreck between two passenger trains gained national attention. The State Fair was held in Mansfield in those days and a special train with 1200 passengers was headed south leaving the fair. Near Butler it met the north bound Chicago Express high-balling through the village. The resulting crash killed 7, and 40 more were badly injured. Doctors were rushed to the scene and local people rendered what assistance they could.

In rolling stock the Lake Erie Division only had 9 engines, 211 freight cars, and 18 passenger, mail, and baggage cars in 1872. By comparison, the Central Ohio Division had 31 engines, 351 freight, and 28 passenger & mail. The former SM&N engines would probably run out their life on their old road, though passenger and freight trains may have been run with B&O engines from the Central Ohio division. The B&O was building their own engines (21 in 1871), and would use their own 4-6-0 Camel back freight engines for years. The B&O had 335 locomotives in 1871, 55 passenger, and 280 freight.

The B&O needed a more direct line from Pittsburg to Chicago, and work on the new road from the Lake Erie Division west was surveyed in 1871-72. The original route was to be west from Havana, through Tiffin, Fostoria, to Deshler. Surveys demonstrated that a terminal further south than Havana would be more practical, especially when the line would be extended east to Pittsburg. Work was started in Fostoria in the spring of 1873 with contractors working in both directions. The line was finished from what was being named Chicago Junction to Deshler by December. The first temporary station at Chicago Junction was an old box car, and it was said that if a man wandered to far into the woods he could get lost.

Fig. 35. The Chicago Junction Station (Willard) was built in 1875. Note the Camel Back engines on the left and wooden box cars to the right. Photo Courtesy of the Willard B&O Museum.

By November of 1874 the new direct route was open from Chicago Junction to Chicago. It was known as the Baltimore and Ohio and Chicago Railroad. Not until 1891 would the eastern line be finished from Chicago Junction to Pittsburg. This line was known as the Akron and Chicago Junction Railroad. B&O built both, with all traffic controlled from Newark until 1902.

The new line was completed so quickly in 1873 that the necessary shops, depot buildings, water stations, and side tracks were not completed until the following year. The B&O purchased 40 acres at Chicago Junction and President Garrett reported on October 1, 1875 that, *one half of a round house for 32 engines, and a machine and blacksmith shop, 70 by 150 feet are being erected.* Also being built was a new depot, *a convenient and substantial structure, combining every convenience for dining and waiting rooms, with sleeping rooms for guests desiring to lie over, will be completed during the coming month.* These were substantial brick structures with slate roofs. Coal chutes with pockets for coal storage were also under construction, as was a reservoir for water. A new double wire telegraph line was run 262 miles from Baltimore Junction to Chicago Junction.

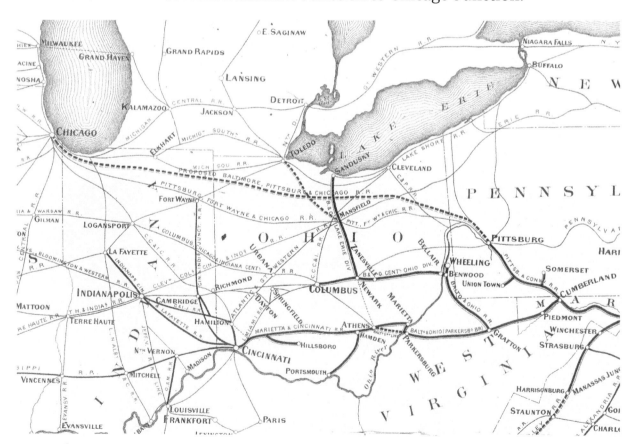

Fig. 36. The 1870 B&O railroad map shows the connecting and competing rail lines. Note that the line south from Newark was not finished.

Another new passenger depot was nearing completion at Newark. Designed for the comfort and convenience of passengers it aided the, *prompt movement of passenger trains at this important station*. The division offices were housed in the imposing two story brick building that was to be a Newark landmark for more than 100 years. It was located at the junction of the Central Ohio and Lake Erie Division yards.

Fig 37. A train load of Aultman Taylor threshing machines was headed west on B&O in 1878. The machines were built in Mansfield. Photo courtesy the Coleman Collection, Ohio Historical Society.

On the Lake Erie Division nearly 3,000 tons of new rails were laid, and additional side tracks added. The passenger station at Mansfield was moved to the junction of the Atlantic & Great Western Railroad, and enlarged for use by both companies. The only other improvement was the construction of a grain elevator and new passenger station at Butler.

The Lake Erie Division appeared to be in good shape, but was still not highly profitable. With the opening of the Chicago line its earnings slowly declined due partly to reconstruction costs. After paying the rental in 1878, the B&O had a net balance of $14,764. By that time the Lake Erie Division had 35 engines, 13 passenger, 14 mail & baggage cars, and 684 freight cars.

A large amount of coal was going north over the road, part of which was destined for the B&O yards at Chicago Junction, which was renamed "Willard" in 1917 after the roads President, Daniel Willard. The Post Office was having trouble differentiating between Chicago and Chicago Junction.

The old SM&N wooden covered bridges would slowly give way to stronger modern iron structures, but even one of these would go down during the flood of February 2, 1883, which also washed away the Bellville station and inundated parts of Mt. Vernon and Newark. Two locks were washed away on the Ohio & Erie Canal, spelling the end of its usefulness. The railroads had nearly put it out of business anyway.

Heavy rains on frozen ground caused sever flooding along the southern portion of the Lake Erie Division, particularly along the Clear Fork of the Mohican and also the Kokosing and Licking Rivers.

Train number 16, in three sections due to the steep grade north of Lexington, was headed out of Newark for Chicago Junction. The trains were slowed by high water near Fredericktown and were due to pass Bellville at 11:00 PM. The first section did

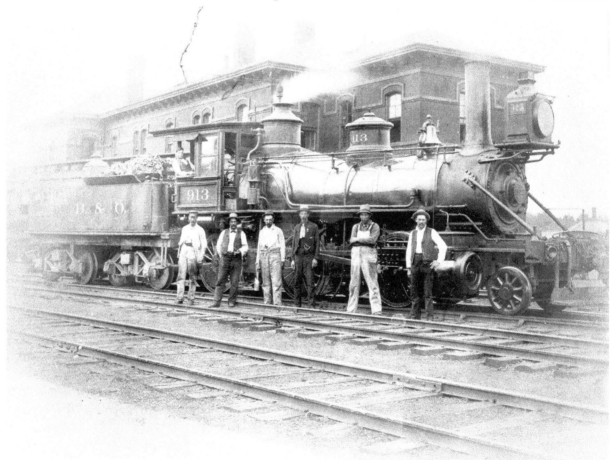

Fig. 38. B&O engine 913, a 2-6-0 built by Danforth in 1873, was photographed next to the Willard station in 1896. Photo Courtesy the Coleman Collection, Ohio Historical Society.

Fig. 39. Passenger engine 890, built by Baldwin in 1892, is shown on the turn table at Willard roundhouse in 1895. The gleaming paint suggests that it has just been out shopped. Note the wood arm that was used to turn the table manually. Photo Courtesy the Coleman Collection, Ohio Historical Society.

not arrive at Bellville until 4:00 AM, and passed safely over the new double span bridge east of town. When the second section crossed things didn't feel right, and a flag-man was sent back to stop the third section. He waited at the east end of the bridge but the engineer didn't see him in time to whistle down brakes. As soon as camelback locomotive #305 was on the bridge the center pier gave way and both sections of the bridge went down along with the engine and six cars.

The engineer and fireman were able to swim and save themselves by climbing the side of the engine and one side of the bridge structure. The front brakeman was crushed between two cars and swept away in the swirling water. His body had not been found a year later despite searches by friends and family.

In the mean time the Bellville station washed away when flood waters undermined it. It was a pile of kindling after it hit a highway bridge on its way downstream.

After a time the first and second sections of number 16 continued on, but the first section developed a hot box north of Mansfield near Springmill. It stopped, and before the second section could be flagged it rammed the first. The caboose and four cars were *smashed to splinters and the engine smashed beyond recognition and lay in a helpless mass upturned in a ditch.* None of the three sections of train number 16 made it to Chicago Junction unharmed.

Later, a crewman on the wreck train from Sandusky, tried to climb aboard the locomotive as it was leaving the wreck scene at Springmill, missed his footing and had one leg crushed. A few days later heavy rains again visited and the B&O suspended all train traffic for 24 hours. A bridge went down at St. Louisville, and loaded coal cars were parked on the temporary bridge at Bellville to help hold it in place. All and all it was a bad week on the B&O.

The Lake Erie division was controlled from Newark, not Chicago Junction. Its central location between the Central Ohio, Lake Erie, and the Straitsville Divisions, made Newark a railroad town, and the B&O was to become the largest employer in Licking County. Over the years the Sandusky yards and car shops were destined to become more of a terminal than a vital part of the railroad, partly due to limited land available for expansion. Some maintenance was being shifted south to Chicago Junction (Willard) and Newark. However, in February of 1883 the Mt. Vernon newspaper noted that, *Master Mechanic Beckert, of the B&O shops at Sandusky, has turned out a new passenger engine, the 513, which he calls "The Flying Dutchman," and claims it can get away from any engine on the road.*

Fig. 40. The Newark Station housed B&O Division Offices in addition to passenger and freight accommodations. The track turning to the right was the beginning of the old SN&N line north. Photo Carl T. Winegardner collection.

The machine shop and car repair facility was still humming along, employing 130 to 150 men. At the same time it was reported that the Newark car builders shop finished a baggage coach that was described as being, *56 feet in the clear, the same size as passenger coaches.* It was for local use, #1 and #8 runs. Newark shops had also been turning out freight cars from 30,000 up to 50,000 pound capacity on a regular basis.

Fig.41. Engine 654 was built in 1874 and photographed in 1891. A year later, a driving rod broke loose, cut the wooden cab in half, killing the engineer Walter Bramble. Railroading was a dangerous business. Photo Courtesy the Willard B&O Museum.

Fig. 42. The second (1885) grain elevator and coal dock at Sandusky. Note the dredge, tug boat and tall ship to the right. The stacked lumber was on the east Lumber and Ore Dock. Photo courtesy Hayes Presidential Library.

The Newark yards also built a *Lost Baggage* building in 1883. That novel idea must have been adopted by airlines in the next century and taken to an extreme beyond imagination. Who would ever think of looking for their airline luggage in Scottsboro, Alabama? Where ever in the hell that is.

The Sandusky grain warehouse burned down in 1883. A new 80,000 bushel capacity building on an improved dock was finished and in operation a year later. There were three docks jutting out into the bay. The west dock had the freight warehouse; center was for grain and coal, and the east for lumber and ore.

In 1882 ore unloading machinery was installed on the B&O ore pier at Sandusky. These giant *Beckert* unloaders were the earliest on the lake ports, and greatly reduced the time and labor involved in unloading ore carriers. A newspaper account states tonnage on the B&O increased from 18,000 in 1880 to 110,000 in 1884, as the cargo could go directly from ship to waiting rail cars. As ships grew bigger and heavier, the shallow harbor and rocks created problems which resulted in traffic shifting to Huron or Lorain. Ore shipments to Sandusky ended by 1910.

There is no exact record of the B&O engines used on the Lake Erie Branch. Old photographs

Fig. 43. From B&O's timetable of December 19, 1880. At this time the Chicago-New York cars wer routed east through Newark, Ohio, and Wheeling, West Virginia. B&O Museum Collection. Cart T. Winegardner

Fig. 44. Winans Camel Back engine #65. These were notorious track jumpers, and if upset, crewman who rode beside the boiler were lucky to escape. The fireman worked stooped under the canopy between the engine and tender. Photo courtesy of the Coleman Collection, Ohio Historical Society.

reveal that in addition to the old SM&N engines, B&O Camel Back engines of two types were used primarily on freights.

The *Winans* 0-8-0 eight-wheel Camels were the oldest, built before and during the early part of the Civil War. They were built for the B&O by Ross Winans, and gained a reputation as notorious track jumpers, averaging one a week. Henry Tyson, Master of Machinery for the B&O, wanted a 10 wheel engine, 4-6-0, with a front truck to guide the locomotive around curves. This Winans refused to build, and the argument went into the company records.

> *...to ride an 8 wheeled Camel engine at a rate of 12 to 15 miles per hour, it will almost pitch you off with its straight forward tendency and stiff connection to all wheels. It will not follow a curve like a 10 wheel engine with her truck and center pin, but will press straight forward, and if the flanges of the wheels, or the wheels themselves, or the track is not sufficiently strong enough to follow the engine from the outside of a curve (which is only done by sudden jerks and concussions), and if not all sufficiently strong enough to withstand these shocks, they must eventually leave the track, which is often the case.*

> *The 10 wheel engine will, with its vibrating truck in front, run the same curve with perfect ease....To take one of these (Winans) Camel engines out of the shop in perfect order, they cannot be run more than 3 or 4 trips before their side-rods and main boxes thump sufficiently to tear the whole side off the engine. Owing to the solid construction of the side rods, they must be taken down a refitted with new brasses, which generally throws the whole strain on the side rods and crank pins, and the brasses are cut out before they run 200 miles. The 10 wheel engines with their adjustable side rods will run from 8 to 10 months before the least thump can be heard.*

> *I have never known a 10 wheel to run off the track thru the fault of the engine. They do not use as much fuel and are more reliable on the road. It is rare to see a 10 wheel leak at its furnace while the (Winans) Camels have to be caulked almost every trip.*

Winans refused to build 10 wheel Camels for the B&O, closed his shop, and never built another locomotive. Bullheaded. Just plain Bullheaded. The B&O had started building their own engines including numerous "Davis" Camels from 1869 to 1873, some of which were still in use at the turn of the century. Most were from the Mt. Clare Shops in Baltimore, which turned out a variety of locomotives.

Newark survived a bitter railroad strike in 1877. The trouble swept across most of the B&O, and lives were lost from Pittsburg to Chicago and elsewhere. Trains were sidetracked by force at Newark, and rioting broke out. Governor Thomas Young called out troops from Cincinnati and Dayton to restore order, and after a period cooler heads prevailed. Fortunately no lives were lost in the Newark area, but the affair left hard feelings for years.

By 1888 employment had reached 550 in the Newark Yards. The B&O employed *"machinist, molders, pattern makers, blacksmiths, cooper smiths, trimmers and car builders....* More men were employed as bridge builders and for track maintenance. It was reported that employment would reach 1,200 men when planned expansion was completed. Labor and material at Newark Yards amounted to $750,000 in 1888. The B&O had become Newark and Licking County's largest employer.

Fig. 45. A 10-wheel Davis Camel #241, built by the B&O at Mt. Clare shops in 1872, Engineer J. Arthur Helms, fireman Neil Floyd. The picture was taken at Chicago Junction (Willard) in 1886. These were good engines with some still in use at the turn of the century. Photo courtesy of the Coleman collection, Ohio Historical Society.

Chapter 16

The Sale of the SM&N

The B&O kept renewing its lease of the old SM&N with minor revisions through the years. On January 17, 1901, the *Sandusky Register* carried a story under the headline, *B&O Officials Elected to Manage S.M. & N.* It detailed the curtain call for Ohio's second oldest railroad:

> *By formal action of the stockholders and newly elected directors Wednesday, the Sandusky, Mansfield & Newark Railroad became part of the B&O. True, it has been operated as such for years, and has actually been owned and controlled by the great system for months, but with the action taken at the annual meeting, the old officers and leading stockholders stepped down and out, to be succeeded by B&O officials.*

> *The meeting was held at the Moss National Bank. Quite a party of B&O officials came up in the private car "Muskingum," of David Lee, superintendent of maintenance of way. The following were elected directors of the SM&N;*

> *Franklin Ames, Chicago, John Q Cowen, Baltimore, J. H. Collins, Columbus, T. J. Trazler, Zanesville, David Lee, Zanesville, James Reynolds, Mansfield, Lincoln Richards, Chicago, P. E. Werner, Akron, C. W. Wolford, Baltimore.*

> *All of the directors are B&O men. John K. Cowen, the new president, is president of the B&O, Judge T. J. Trazler is chief counsel. The change is a result of reorganization of the B&O, Mr. Jay O. Moss and John Gardiner, having disposed of their holdings. The road is now owned and controlled by the B&O.*

John Gardiner was 85, a very wealthy banker from Norwalk, had served as a director or former board member of three Ohio railroads including the Sandusky Mansfield & Newark, where he had served as President in 1870 and beyond after the death of C. L. Boalt. Evidently he and Jay Moss bought up most of the remaining stock over the years, possibly as the original investors died or developed other interests. At 85, he had outlived most of them and was 98 when he died.

Jay O. Moss was President of the Moss National Bank in Sandusky, which had been founded in 1863 by his father. It was, in part, a family institution with a number of officers and directors being members of the Moss family. Apparently they too had collected SM&N stock, and the reorganization of the B&O prompted disposal of all SM&N stock. Jay Moss had served as Vice President of the SM&N, and died in 1911.

Although the Sandusky Mansfield & Newark would still exist on paper for financial reasons, for all practical purposes it was the end of a railroad that had never really been profitable until it was leased to the Baltimore & Ohio controlled Central Ohio Railroad. Ironically, it was John Gardiner who had helped arrange that union. Unfortunately many disappointed investors had gone to their graves with little to show for their investments, or their faith in building a better Ohio.

Fig. 46. South bound passenger #4. Note the station agent ready with freight wagon.

Chapter 17

What Remains in 2002

A tornado on June 28, 1924, destroyed the B&O round house, warehouses, and support buildings on the Sandusky waterfront. The whole waterfront was in shambles. The city water tower was blown over and the pumping station heavily damaged. Many houses and business buildings were wrecked. The National Guard was called in by the Governor to assist in helping the injured and maintain order. The B&O rushed 30 men from Zanesville for relief and labor, and offered use of the rail line and facilities for what ever purpose needed. Many of the B&O buildings were never replaced.

A bronze plaque in a small waterfront park marks the spot where the three piers jutted out into the bay. It states that the last time the B&O used the docks was in 1973. No buildings remain where the round house complex was located, although you can still see where the tracks went down Warren Street. A side track went down Water Street past the boat docks and factory district. The shore line has given way to pleasure boating and high rise apartments. It's a beautiful part of the city.

The tracks were taken up between Willard and Sandusky in the early 1980s. Following the old line south Slate Run Station (where the ivory like tusk was unearthed) was evidently within the confines of the NASA Plum Brook Station. The railroad was rerouted around the vast acreage when a munition manufacturing facility was built there during World War Two. The railroad turned to the south-west at Wilmer and rejoined the old bed just south of Prout. Anything that marked the location of Slate Run Station undoubtedly fell to bulldozers.

Prout, or Huron Station as it was earlier called, is located on Mason Road about a mile east of Bloomingville. A marvelous piece of Americana, Stanley's Tavern, (where you can get something to drink and a super chopped sirloin sandwich) is located across the roadbed from a country grain elevator and feed mill. That's the whole town. The station was across the road from the tavern. No evidence is visible of the old Huron Branch.

Monroeville was where the old Cleveland & Toledo line crossed the SM&N. A couple of buildings remain at the intersection, but it is not known whether they were former B&O. The old abandon interconnect road beds, and remains of the electric rail lines are visible.

Two abandoned rail bridges cross the Huron River, and a sign indicates that a bike trail on an old roadbed is planned. Something like that between Sandusky and Monroeville on the old SM&N would be a welcome tourist attraction for both cities. It's an interesting junction in a town that still has many old buildings from the 1850s and 60s.

Nothing remains of Pontiac, which was located at the junction of State Route 99 and Sand Hill Roads. The abutments of the stone arch bridge are to be seen to the south in the long fill at Pontiac Section Line Road. According to a local resident, the county sent a crew out with a back hoe to tear them out to widen the road. After a day of banging away they gave up and left. The railroad built things to last.

Fig. 47. The former Daily Brothers General Store in Havana. A siding went along the building. A warehouse at the rear has been torn down.

The brick store of the Dailey Brothers is still standing in Havana, well preserved and little changed, although the warehouse which was attached to the rear along the tracks was torn down. The Dailey's bought the building in 1870 from a man named Hayes, and the building no doubt dates from the 1850s. A side track ran along side the store. It's a pleasant crossroads community located east of State Route 99 on Greenfield Road.

Centerton is another small cluster of houses. It was named by the Mansfield & Sandusky City Railroad because it was half way between those two cities. The county history states its 71 ½ feet above Havana and 295 feet above Lake Erie. The raised roadbed cuts through the place, but nothing remains of railroad structures. It's east of Route 99 about 2 miles on Egypt Rd.

Willard was the junction of the Lake Erie and the Chicago lines of the B&O. The once considerable collection of brick buildings and the round house from the early B&O ownership have all been torn down. What remains is the nearly 2 mile long yards, two pumping station operations, a fueling depot, and recent cement block office building. Across town to the west is the B&O Museum and Park. Inside, when it's open (there's a shortage of volunteers), is a wonderful collection of B&O photographs, artifacts, and displays relating to Willard and its connection to the B&O, which was its life blood for more than a century. It's well worth the time to visit. Your best bet is Sunday afternoons in summer.

Although the tracks from Willard to Sandusky have been removed, the CSX line south from Willard to Mansfield remains. Nothing is to be seen at Shelby Junction, and only a small metal building on East Main Street in Shelby is still usable by train crews. Coal is delivered to the power plant and sidings into the old Air Force Depot are still in place but little used by local industries. This was a busy place during World War Two.

The Plymouth B&O station building has survived, and was moved to a different location by a local industrial plant. For a while it was used by the Fate Root Heath Company, which among other things built small industrial railroad locomotives. The deep cut through Plymouth was the location of Burr Higgins warehouse that collapsed over the tracks. It was just west of the town square.

Houses, and the old spring-fed mill building (it's now a home) at Springmill remain. It's hard to believe that the railroad even stopped here, let alone owned a boarding house.

The CSX delivers cars from Willard to Mansfield where the State-assisted Ashland Railroad picks them up. The CSX, Conrail, and old Erie lines all merge in the valley on North Main Street. The Ashland Railroad uses the CSX and the Erie rails to serve customers in both Mansfield and Ashland. It's interesting to try to figure out where everything goes. The AK Steel plant, and Mansfield grain elevators, are the biggest customers for the Ashland Railroad and Con Rail. Norfolk and Western, the only through line left, serves the Ontario GM facility.

Oak Hill Cottage, the former home of John Robinson, 1850s board member and superintendent of the SM&N, has been restored and is open for weekend tours. It's just off Springmill St. in Mansfield and overlooks the old rail line in the industrial valley below. It's an interesting home with many original furnishings.

In the spring of 1987 the CSX began taking up the rails between Mansfield and Butler. The last train of cars passed on April 1st, and by the 22nd of the month the tracks were up between Mansfield and Lexington. The removal continued south thru Bellville to Butler, and later between Butler and Fredericktown. The

Fig. 48. A brakeman was killed in this head on collision in Bellville in November 1900. The Engineer of the south bound freight failed to correctly understand his orders and neglected to pull into Shafer's siding. The conductor realized the mistake and succeeded in uncoupling the caboose and several cars. The brakeman, for some reason, started forward on his engine and was crushed between the two locomotives.

Mansfield to Butler section was purchased for use as a bike trail and paved with State and Federal funds after considerable legal haggling and fussing by land owners. It has been a well proven, and much used, asset to Richland County. It's a shame it hasn't been extended to Fredericktown. A similar bike trail from Sandusky to Monroeville would help both towns with tourists business.

Alta, the small station at the *summit* is only marked by a keen eye to detect the *Y* for turning cars and engines. A good guess is that after the turn table at Mansfield was abandoned, possibly due to space requirements as engines grew and real-estate became more expensive, the *Y* was built at Alta. Engines from Newark could turn around at this point and go back south to help the next train. Located on Marion Avenue, the Alta Greenhouse stands where the station was located.

The station at Lexington has survived due to heroic efforts by the local men's group and local elected officials. The railroad had been renting the building to the Kiwanis Club for community use for a number of years, but was bound and determined to tear it down. After much negotiating, the building was saved and enlarged. It is now a much used Senior Center and an asset to the village.

Bellville and Butler did not fare as well. Community leaders sat on their rears as both towns watched their station disappear. The only possible railroad structure remaining might be the old grain elevators. B&O records state that an elevator was built in Butler in 1875. The center section of the present elevator in Butler appears to be of that age. Unknown is the possibly that the one in Bellville might share the same background.

Fig. 49. The Hunt's mill station – general store.

The CSX still uses the tracks from Newark to Fredericktown. Most of the freight business is in Mt. Vernon, but cars are seen in Fredericktown from time to time. The B&O Station in Mt. Vernon is still intact but showing neglect. The

brick building with a
red tile roof is a dis-
tinctive feature in a
town known for its
architecture. It's a
shame it hasn't been
restored and put to
some   commercial
or civic use. Perhaps
it will be yet saved
from the wrecker's
ball. It needs to be
done soon.

Fig. 50. The old B&O pile driver still banging away in 1911.

Hunts Station is about 4 miles south of Mt. Vernon and a mile west of State Route
13 on Sycamore Road. The large house-like two story structure appears to have
been partially remodeled and is undergoing slow restoration. It's unusual to find
this size station in such a rural area. Old-timers down the road claim it was a general store and also rented rooms on the second floor. A large porch on the track
side was for passengers who could buy tickets from the station agent at the store.
A long side track has been removed, and an old section building is still standing
across the road which also at one time had stock pens and loading facilities.

Utica saved their station through the efforts of the local Sertoma Club, and put
it to a new community use. The distinctive architecture is a reminder of the
various styles used by the B&O over the years. It's one of the classic designs
not usually found. The town deserves credit for preserving many of its old down
town buildings. Although remodeled and resided, it evidently was built sometime
around the turn of the century.

 St. Louisville and Vanatta have railroad bridges over the Licking River, and it's
interesting to see where so many SM&N structures were lost in floods. The stream
does not appear to be large, but the absence of houses indicates the flood level.
Several former freight buildings are still along the road bed, as is an old B&O horse
car, designed just for hauling horses. St. Louisville had a population of about 150
in 1869 and Vannatta's was listed as being a signal station.

Newark has shared about the same fate as Willard. The rail yard remains but the
round house, car buildings, freight house, and imposing station are all gone. They even

tore down the lost luggage building! The sharp curve out of the yard north was the beginning of the old SM&N. According to Carl T. Winegardner, retired B&O conductor writer and historian, the curve limited engine size such that nothing larger than a Q3 Baldwin Light Mikado was permitted on the line, although the writer can remember seeing at least one Q4 Heavy Mike. The yard and nearby manufacturing museum are interesting places to visit. A couple of small office and maintenance buildings stand guard over what once was Licking County's largest employer.

Fig. 51. The Mt. Vernon station is still standing but in need of a new owner and much repair. This photo is dated 1901. Photo courtesy Carl T. Winegardner.

Fig. 52. End of the Line! An old Winans camel being cut up for scrap in 1893. Bought in 1863, its boiler had exploded in 1872 killing the engineer and fireman.

SANDUSKY, MANSFIELD & NEWARK LOCOMOTIVES
All engines were built by Rogers

Name	Date	Type	Build #	Cylinder and Wheels
Mansfield	10/44	4-4-2	59	10 ½ x 18--54
Empire	7/45	4-4-0	69	12 x 18--54
Vigilance	5/45	2-2-0	70	6 x 18--60
Knox	6/46	4-2-0	84	11 x 18 --54
Licking	10/46	4-2-0	92	12 ½ x 22--72
Richland	4/47	4-4-2?	98	11 x 18 -- 54
Bellville	6/48	4-2-0	132	12 ½ x 22 --54
Newark	50	4-4-0		
Plymouth	3/51	4-4-0	253	13 x 20 -- 60
Lexington	3/51	4-4-0	254	13 x 20 -- 60
Independence	4/51	4-4-0	255	13 x 20 -- 60
Utica	4/51	4-4-0	256	13 x 20 -- 60
Frederick	8/51	4-4-0	273	15 x 20 -- 60
Shelby	8/51	4-4-0	274	15 x 20 -- 60
Sandusky	9/51	4-4-0	277	15 x 20 -- 60
Mohican	7/53	4-6-0	405	17 x 22 -- 54
Hocking	7/53	4-6-0	407	17 x 22 -- 54
Erie	10/55			16 x 20 -- ?
Mt. Vernon	11/55			16 x 18 -- ?
Newark (2nd)	1/64	4-4-0	1134	16 x 22 -- 60
Mansfield (2nd)	1/64	4-4-0	1136	16 x 22 -- 60
Frederick (2nd)	3/64	4-4-0	1144	16 x 22 -- 60
Monroeville	3/64	4-4-0	1146	16 x 22 -- 60

Fig 53. The Annual Report for 1857 states that "the engine "Jerry Myers" is estimated to cost $1,500 to put in running order". No other information has been found as to type or manufacture. It's possible that it was bought used, perhaps from Cooper & Clark, or some other railroad.

Reprinted with permission from "Steam Locomotives of the Baltimore an Ohio" by William D. Edson.

TAB

Classified Statement of the different kinds of Freight transported over S.,

1868.	BUSHELS.						BARRELS.						
RECEIVED AT.	Wheat.	Oats.	Corn.	Rye.	Barley	Seeds.	Flour.	Whisky and High Wines.	Pork.	Eggs.	Salt.	Plaster and Cement.	Fish.
Sandusky,	13,656	7,110	11,968			64	2,748	579	20	3	69		127
Monroeville,	11,550	11,370	1,908	810	10,044	92	22		3	143	222	290	2
Havana,			285								275	52	25
Centerton,			32				5	5			306	12	31
New Haven,							14	1	2		101	5	7
Plymouth,						152					730	106	37
Shelby Junction,	385	19,798	14,516	1,984	1,179	1,371	1,576		47	3,302	7	94	437
Shelby,			350			122	63	13			398	44	120
Mansfield,	6,647	31,712	32,500	10,762	1,264	3,331	1,768	344	111	13,530	9,500	2,748	1,847
Lexington,											352	117	109
Belleville,										55	276	197	90
Independence,		111	141			40		2			278	188	26
Ankenytown,							1				46	27	2
Frederick,											669	167	162
Mt. Vernon,	790					4,036	3,775	168	1	349	3,801	1,035	408
Hunt's,							118				200		1
Utica,							688				540	62	4
St Louisville,							40			25	120	65	
Newark,	79,359	14,960	15,897	8,407	7,691	1,659	3,346		95	54	1,053	1,932	12,497
Totals 1868,	112,387	85,061	77,597	21,963	20,178	10,847	14,164	1,112	279	17,461	18,943	7,141	15,932
Totals 1867,	178,279	215,758	153,996	29,346	19,454	17,396	21,943	1,651	897	18,333	16,730	6,514	11,961
FORWARDED FROM													
Sandusky,	370	20	742		15,794	71	1,530	90	105		12,825	7,127	15,847
Monroeville,	22,606		3,044			243	4,771	393	5				
Havana,	2,959	943				25	177			40			
Centerton,						675	1		5	90			1
New Haven,										10			
Plymouth,	21,402	12,394	285	136	659	801			3	35			
Shelby Junction,						183		60	8				3
Shelby,	3,398	9,576				435	67			12			1
Mansfield,	58,081	2,328		1,168	746	397	3,769	23		331		6	41
Lexington,	658	2,316		36		1,377	10		7				
Belleville,	677	3,650		1,648		689	81		2	1,086			
Independence,		2,604		2,649		3,891	239			221			
Ankenytown,		877	332	890	83	255	1			84			
Frederick,	50	4,895	3,866	392	453	444	75		2	832		1	38
Mt. Vernon,	1,501	10,448	11,754	4,567	1,903	1,176	2,424	10	142	10,003	256	7	
Hunt's,		1,537	10,830	93		10							
Utica,		6,793	519	2,221	540	40				2,011			
St. Louisville,			3,570	300			10			645			
Newark,	685	26,680	42,655	7,863		125	999	536		2,061	5,862		1
Totals,	112,387	85,061	77,597	21,963	20,178	10,847	14,164	1,113	279	17,461	18,943	7,141	15,932

☞ Under the head of " Miscellaneous Merchandise," are included all articles not clearly defined in the other columns,

Fig. 54a. Left half of Table F.

LE F.

M. & N. R. R., to and from all Stations during 1868, and Earnings from same.

	POUNDS.			TONS.		CARS.			FEET.	M.	EARNINGS COMPARED.	
Butter.	Lard.	Wool.	Miscella-neous M'd'se.	Coal.	Pig Iron.	Stav's	Stock.	Sun-dries.	Lumber.	Shingles and Lath.	1868.	1867.
3,278	5,815	450,529	4,452,127	2,708	50	102	2	62	713,850	....	$27,268 89	23,792 99
5,874	2,929	29,200	5,432,901	322	3	55	12	22	304,767	350,600	12,250 70	17,033 46
......	270	......	276,492	20	....	3	3	7	45,285	239,500	945 55	958 29
......	......	......	568,324	....	....	2	....	7	13,243	95,000	1,295 98	1,181 73
......	......	......	199,861	....	....	..	....	5	11,490	70,000	506 08	72 23
......	......	1,899	1,044,893	254	4	1	....	52	307,914	894,000	4,487 80	3,611 40
227,859	10,592	845,697	1,779,826	10	47	47	18	6	174,878	345,750	9,140 98	7,048 83
......	......	200	662,652	563	.	5	1	38	372,761	822,500	4,088 52	5,220 16
627,640	14,120	980,012	9,208,577	1,966	284	39	578	289	4,122,963	4,430,250	51,404 94	53,435 88
......	......	......	356,385	40	....	..	....	....	18,456	47,500	1,000 03	1,075 83
2,020	......	......	495,820	90	....	3	....	5	68,390	192,500	1,942 09	1,781 98
......	......	1,000	454,839	60	....	..	....	3	154,404	145,250	1,374 04	1,149 62
......	......	......	50,116	....	....	..	....	....	5,150	30,000	200 53	147 47
......	......	1,899	1,238,033	310	13	....	....	11	156,826	837,000	5,203 21	4,903 32
20,669	317	314	6,687,268	6,791	786	1	1	83	1,040,892	2,574,250	32,858 73	27,767 69
......	......	......	180,862	20	....	..	....	....	20,668	16,000	553 89	313 33
......	......	......	848,231	290	....	2	....	....	105,397	595,400	3,680 79	2,621 96
1,405	......	......	123,757	200	8	....	....	33	29,000	109,000	507 89	394 97
38,307	7,048	33,777	8,599,638	10	10	26	4	112	6,769,397	10,577,500	55,960 80	54,787 90
926,452	41,091	2,242,628	42,660,602	13,654	1,205	286	619	735	14,435,731	22,192,000	214,671 42	207,299 04
968,503	253,518	1,782,558	41,803,510	11,601	916	221	677	738	9,711,752	16,441,300		

	403	27,232	3,349,545	299	....	86	1	444	12,885,478	20,988,750	83,097 68	66,309 73
238	2,593	2,350	2,368,805	......	100	2	1	124	66,868	76,000	8,949 25	13,532 61
10,980	579	12,848	145,242	......	....	80	7	4	76,935	....	1,834 14	2,048 21
42,448	......	6,758	598,472	......	....	94	8	14	210,923	....	2,967 25	3,107 49
......	......	......	85,634	......	....	18	....	17	7,000	....	720 92	82 53
11,667	710	217,347	741,532	......	....	4	20	5	172,085	24,800	4,015 03	4,086 29
......	......	......	5,914,808	10	110	....	11	17	486,134	508,250	10,757 58	9,194 11
14,818	2,976	6,349	306,107	......	....	....	....	....	24,774	6,000	1,179 58	2,203 68
691	2,051	23,895	7,939,859	930	142	2	3	7	414,389	562,000	20,512 86	23,896 68
9,422	2,998	47,256	498,295	......	....	..	9	....	66,516	....	1,452 81	1,244 95
73,571	200	83,564	542,875	......	....	..	30	95	7,000	....	2,514 22	3,639 31
8,736	750	33,395	168,926	......	....	..	5	....	400	....	1,074 92	1,706 19
1,972	3,645	......	46,970	......	....	..	....	....	......	....	306 97	531 06
26,894	19,035	228,941	707,989	......	....	..	121	8	......	....	5,505 25	5,429 15
625,736	......	789,583	8,634,715	......	....	..	160	4	9,429	....	20,419 11	21,402 19
......	3,451	16,299	195,081	......	....	..	2	....	......	....	489 82	54 23
60,448	300	232,666	414,293	......	....	..	119	1	6,500	13,000	5,015 00	4,791 00
20,415	......	12,838	38,452	......	....	..	....	....	......	....	508 45	838 63
18,416	1,400	501,307	10,963,002	12,415	853	....	122	65	1,300	14,000	43,350 58	43,200 81
926,452	41,091	2,242,628	42,660,602	13,654	1,205	286	619	735	14,435,731	22,192,000	214,671 42	207,299 04

s, except Stone, Hoop Poles, Lime, Brick, Sand and Ice, which come under the head of "Sundries," in car loads.

Fig. 54b. Right Half of Table F.

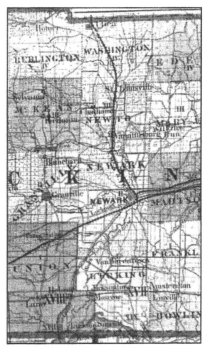

Route of the
SM&N Railroad
from Sandusky to
Newark, Ohio

From H. F. Walling, *Atlas of
the State of Ohio,* 1868

Fig. 55. Route of the SM&N Railroad from Sandusky to Newark, Ohio..

The Author

Robert A. Carter was born in Mansfield, Ohio, in 1935, and graduated from Lexington High School in 1954. Married with 5 children and 10 grandchildren, 3 great grandchildren. He currently lives in Mansfield with his wife Jackie. He is a member of the Richland County Chapter of the Ohio Genealogical Society, the Ohio Historical Society, and the Society for Preservation of Old Mills (SPOOM). Since 1964 he has written six local area history books, including *1964 Lexington Sesquicentennial booklet;* and *The Sandusky Mansfield & Newark Railroad (*2002 and Second Edition, 2024); *Tom Lyons The Indian That Died 13 Times,* 2003; *Tales of the Old-Timers – The History of Lexington(* 2007 and Second Edition, 2023); *The Mansfield Riots of 1900* (2009 and Second Edition, 2024); and *Water-Power Mills of Richland County,* 2016. As of 2024, he continues to write articles for the *Tribune -Courier* in Richland County, Ohio.

Also Available from
Turas Publishing
by Robert A. Carter

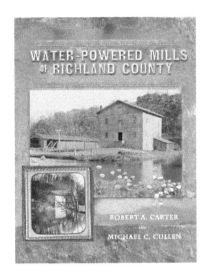

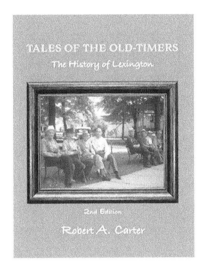

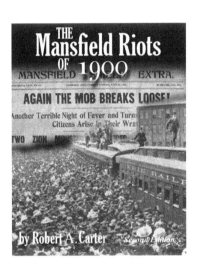

$29.00

$26.00

$25.00

https://turaspublishing.com/product/
water-powered-mills-of-richland-
county/

https://turaspublishing.com/product/
tales-of-the-old-timers/

https://turaspublishing.com/product/
the-mansfield-riots-of-1900/